Comments on other *Amazing Stories* from readers & reviewers

"You might call them the non-fiction response to Harlequin romances: easy to consume and potentially addictive."
Robert Martin, *The Chronicle Herald*

"Tightly written volumes filled with lots of wit and humour about famous and infamous Canadians."
Eric Shackleton, *The Globe and Mail*

"This is popular history as it should be... For this price, buy two and give one to a friend."
Terry Cook, a reader from Ottawa, on **Rebel Women**

"Stories are rich in description, and bristle with a clever, stylish realness."
Mark Weber, *Central Alberta Advisor,* on **Ghost Town Stories II**

"The resulting book is one readers will want to share with all the women in their lives."
Lynn Martel, *Rocky Mountain Outlook,* on **Women Explorers**

"[The books are] long on plot and character and short on the sort of technical analysis that can be dreary for all but the most committed academic."
Robert Martin, *The Chronicle Herald*

"A compelling read. Bertin ... has selected only the most intriguing tales, which she narrates with ⌐ wealth of detail."
Joyce Glasner, *New Brunswick*

"The heightened sense of drama a good dose of human interest is whe
Pamela Klaffke, *C*

D1379059

Working miracles.

WORKING MIRACLES

AMAZING STORIES®

WORKING MIRACLES

The Drama and Passion of Aimee Semple McPherson

BIOGRAPHY

by Judith Robinson

PUBLISHED BY ALTITUDE PUBLISHING CANADA LTD.
1500 Railway Avenue, Canmore, Alberta T1W 1P6
www.altitudepublishing.com
www.amazingstories.ca
1-800-957-6888

Extreme care has been taken to ensure that all information presented in
this book is accurate and up to date. Neither the author nor the
publisher can be held responsible for any errors.

Publisher	Stephen Hutchings
Associate Publisher	Kara Turner
Series Editor	Diana Marshall
Editor	Dianne Smyth
Cover and Layout	Bryan Pezzi

We acknowledge the financial support of the Government
of Canada through the Book Publishing Industry Development
Program (BPIDP) for our publishing activities.

Altitude GreenTree Program
Altitude Publishing will plant twice as many trees as were used
in the manufacturing of this product.

National Library of Canada Cataloguing in Publication Data

Robinson, Judith, 1955-
Working miracles / Judith Robinson.

(Amazing stories)
Includes bibliographical references.
ISBN 1-55439-085-0

1. McPherson, Aimee Semple, 1890-1944. 2. Evangelists--
United States--Biography. 3. International Church of the
Foursquare Gospel--Clergy--Biography. I. Title. II. Series:
Amazing stories (Canmore, Alta.)

BX7990.I68M3 2006   289.9   C2006-900806-X

Printed and bound in Canada by Friesens
2 4 6 8 9 7 5 3 1

Contents

Prologue

Horses clomped by in the Florida mud as the wagons hauled supplies. Voices cried out from every direction while the men grunted and groaned in an effort to quickly erect a row of sleeping tents. There was a sense of excitement and urgency in the air.

Aimee's husband, Harold, usually wired a string of electric bulbs across the top of the structures where she preached, but there was no power line here. So, for the umpteenth time, Aimee struggled to light her calcium carbide lamp. This lamp always gave her trouble when she tried to light it. Harold moved swiftly towards her, as the handful of worshippers at the alter mumbled the unintelligible sounds characteristic of revival tent meetings during World War I. Aimee didn't want to admit to Harold that she couldn't light the lamp. She gave it one last try.

Suddenly, the lamp exploded in her face — sending flames a foot high into the air — singeing her hair, her eyebrows, and her eyelashes. Harold managed to put out the flames with a woollen blanket, and then frantically shoved her head into a nearby barrel of rainwater. At that moment, her pride hurt worse than her face.

The crowd was filling the tabernacle for the evening meeting. When she turned to face them everyone gasped, horrified. She realized that she was badly burned and that she was terrifying her audience. In agony, she slowly dragged herself up to the platform. Her skin was stretched so tight across her mouth that she could barely speak. Aimee cried out for God to heal her.

In the next moment, Harold noticed her skin starting to change colour. The blisters were beginning to disappear. Could it be? He moved closer to his wife to make sure. The blisters were gone. Aimee's face was completely restored.

Chapter 1
Love and Transformation

imee Elizabeth Kennedy had discovered God. Her mother, Minnie, told her it was more like she had discovered a certain Pentecostal preacher. But Aimee was sure it was God. When she prayed Aimee felt an incredible warmth flood over her whole body.

Other 17-year-olds might have preferred to talk about boys, books, clothes, or ambitions, but Aimee only wanted to talk about God. She talked about Him all day long to whoever would listen. Her friends in the drama club began to avoid her. The eggheads at the top of the class no longer asked her opinion about things and began to pull back from her. She had recently begun making the long trek to school and back alone.

But she had made some new friends at the Pentecostal Mission. It was the music that first attracted Aimee to the Pentecostal Church. She could hear the heart-stirring strains halfway down the street. This was even better than the brass bands at the Salvation Army. She loved belting out the hymns at the top of her voice, parading up and down the aisles waving handkerchiefs, and proclaiming her new mission.

Aimee never knew what was going to happen next. The atmosphere at the mission was delicious, radical, and unique. Lame people came in on crutches — and went out leaping — physically healed. Deaf people got their hearing back. This was exciting! Aimee had never seen anything like this at the Salvation Army. People were laughing and dancing, and falling to their knees under the power of God. Aimee loved every minute of it.

Her mother hated it. Pentecostal emotionalism made Minnie so angry that it made Aimee ache to get involved. Anything her mother hated had to be wonderful. Minnie told her daughter that these people spent entirely too much time in prayer and socializing, and not enough time serving others. Hard work was what was required of a dedicated Christian.

James Kennedy, Aimee's father, was a Methodist. He didn't mind his daughter experimenting with other forms of religion. He even took her to the mission once in awhile himself. Aimee's father didn't see anything frightening there. He was 35 years older than his Salvation Army bride, and he had his feet firmly on the ground. Nothing was going to knock him off of his perch. His family had lived for generations on the same farm in Salford, outside London, Ontario. His roots were firm and deep. Age had given him a more liberal view of humanity and its shortcomings.

Neither of her parents realized just how serious Aimee was about the Pentecostal movement, until she began to skip school to go and pray with her friends. Aimee had been at the top of her class. She was the one her teachers had called upon to answer the questions and she was the one they had counted on to always have her homework done.

Not anymore. Aimee spent all of her time in prayer — seeking the baptism of the Holy Spirit — and firmly convinced that speaking in tongues was real. People had been speaking in tongues in North America for less than 10 years before the handsome young Robert Semple and his friends introduced it to the town of Ingersoll. Minnie, on the other hand, thought that this was ridiculous. She couldn't imagine people allowing their tongues to form gibberish and then trying to pass it off as messages from on high.

Aimee believed that Ingersoll might be one of the first places in Canada to receive this blessing and she was not going to miss out on it. Aimee didn't want to miss out on anything exciting. She was open, susceptible, and eager, and she dared God to let her have everything He had to offer. Robert Semple told Aimee that he had known people in the United States who had been given languages by God, real languages such as Chinese or Russian. He knew this to be true because people who had never heard these languages before were suddenly giving messages from God to people in their own foreign languages.

To Aimee, this sounded wonderful. She wanted God to use her in that way. Night after night, she prayed on her knees at the homes of her Pentecostal friends, begging God to make her a miracle worker. One night, after Aimee had been on her knees for hours in the basement of a friend's home, she felt heat envelop her body and she began to tremble uncontrollably. Then, suddenly, she felt light-headed and a bit dizzy. When she tried to call out for her friend she couldn't get the words out — her tongue felt thick, fuzzy —strange sounds began to emerge from her throat.

Although she tried to communicate in English, the words eventually tumbled out in another tongue. She tried to get up and fell back onto her knees. Her legs were weak and she was overcome by an intense heat, almost as if she had a fever. She felt giddy and happy and she began to laugh. This must be the baptism that she had so long been seeking! This was the presence of the Holy Spirit taking over her tongue and using it to communicate with God, in a language only He could understand.

When Robert Semple ran down the stairs he saw a woman transformed. His little friend Aimee was so much more joyful than he had ever seen her. She was radiant and her features seemed softer and more feminine, vulnerable, yet gentle.

Always quick to talk, Aimee was now speechless, smiling and laughing and crying at the same time. Then she babbled a few words in a language he couldn't understand. When he hugged her he felt the true presence of the power of God. He had never seen anyone receive the baptism in the Holy Spirit like this. Surely this was a sign that God had special things in store for her.

The next day, Aimee tried to describe her experience to her parents but they did not understand. Although her devout Salvation Army mother had dedicated her daughter to God's service, when Aimee was born in Salford, Ontario, on October 9, 1890, she hadn't expected God to take the dedication quite so literally. To Minnie, the dedication was a symbolic gesture. She wanted her daughter to grow up to be a respectable, hardworking, decent citizen, not a fanatical lunatic. How could she snatch her daughter back from God's clutches, without appearing to be a total hypocrite?

James looked at the situation quite cynically, as he did most things. His attitude was that her Pentecostal obsession would soon pass. He was pleased his daughter was excited about something, and the Holy Spirit wasn't a bad thing to get excited about. He was glad she was happy, and he encouraged Aimee to keep moving in any direction that brought her joy. He never confronted the deeper realities of what she was experiencing. He just shrugged it off as youthful zest, and was glad that Aimee wasn't indulging in something more dangerous.

Minnie was annoyed with James. She believed that he never took anything seriously, and that he wasn't thinking clearly and logically enough to help his daughter out of her deep pit. Minnie couldn't get him riled up enough to do anything. He just milked the cows, went on long walks, muttered to himself and sat out on the porch with a pleasant smile on his face. Minnie had looked up to James when she first met him in 1886. When she was 15 years old she had come to the farm in Salford to care for James' dying wife. Minnie had grown up in the small town of Lindsay, hundreds of kilometres to the north, and when her parents died, she had no choice but to go out and earn a living. At first she was grateful for the attentions and affections of the gentle man who, sometime after his wife died, had become her husband. He had a certain strength of character as well as maturity and wisdom. But years later, the 35 years between them became an unbearable chasm.

James was 71 years old. He wanted to sit on the porch and coast till the end of his days. But Minnie, at 36, was just beginning to build up steam. She didn't want to sit around on an isolated farm for the rest of her days, and she didn't want to have to raise her out-of-control daughter on her own. Her anger at James was smouldering and would soon become red hot. Why didn't he do anything to help his daughter? Couldn't he see that she was disappearing into a thick fanatical fog out of which she might never reappear? In Minnie's view James didn't even seem to care. He was in a fog of his own, otherwise known as "aging." Minnie thought she was the only one in the family who could cope with hard cold reality head on.

Aimee didn't mind her parent's bickering. She was used to it. They were never really nasty to each other. They just took their own separate paths, her mother the Salvation Army and her father the farm. They didn't have much in common, but they didn't dislike each other either. Aimee had never seen her mother quite so angry with her father as she was after Aimee tried to explain the baptism of the Holy Spirit to the two of them.

Her father refused to condemn it or to speak out against it, while her mother went ballistic. Minnie ranted, raved, and screamed in an effort to make James yell back. But he never did. Time after time his reaction was simply to walk away from her. He would go down to the pasture or out onto the porch until Minnie calmed down. He never held a grudge and he never got upset.

Aimee could see they thought she was a little crazed, but she didn't care. Robert understood her and he was her mentor now, not her parents. Her parents no longer had much control over her, as she knew that God, and his servant Robert, were guiding her. Aimee and Robert spent hours together walking along the peaceful country roads. The weeping willows and the oak trees took on a special glow when Robert was explaining the scriptures or telling Aimee about the wonders of God's creation. Robert was good-natured and kind and he taught her things she had never been taught in the Salvation

Army — how to listen to God's voice — and how to surrender to the guidance of the Holy Spirit.

A few months after they met, Robert proposed marriage. Seventeen didn't seem too young to be married. Aimee's mother had married at 15. Besides, she would have the best husband anyone could ask for. Robert was over six feet tall, with wavy hair and sparkling mischievous blue eyes, and he had a great sense of humour. When he told stories in his Irish brogue, Aimee felt like she was going to faint dead out. They were married on her parent's farm in August 1908. Aimee had never been more radiant. She was sure she was doing the right thing, and that God's blessing was on both of them. She couldn't imagine how anyone could be happier. Her husband was a preacher, but not just an ordinary preacher, a Pentecostal preacher. Robert Semple heard the voice of God — and miracles occurred when he preached — actual physical healings. Before Robert came into her life, Aimee had never seen a true miracle. She was mesmerized.

After working for a few months as a labourer, Robert told Aimee that God had told him to go to China as a missionary. Aimee was three months pregnant, and she didn't think this was a good time to leave Canada, but if this was God's will, how could she say no? They had no money, but they were both convinced that God would provide. Robert managed to gather enough money from their supporters in southern Ontario to pay for their passage on the *Empress of Ireland*. It was June 1910 by the time they reached Hong Kong. A crowd was waiting to meet them, as the resident missionaries were extremely happy to have reinforcements.

It wasn't easy being a missionary in the Far East at the beginning of the twentieth century. All the Christian denominations had bonded together for strength and community. The young couple soon began to realize that the missionaries stood together in order to survive. They helped the Semples locate an apartment next to a Hindu temple where Aimee heard sounds she had never heard before, like chanting, moaning, and a wailing kind of music. Aimee struggled to adjust to the clattering sounds, the strong smells, and the unfamiliar foods, but most of all to the intense and relentless heat.

The Semples immediately began language lessons in Cantonese. Aimee had never found it hard to learn new things, although the information didn't usually stay with her for very long. The Cantonese pronunciations were easy for her but the words were quickly forgotten. Robert, meanwhile, struggled to get his tongue around the language but, unfortunately, he didn't make much headway either.

Nevertheless, every day Robert went out on the street and tried to mingle with the locals. He tried to win the Chinese over by smiling and gesturing, bartering for food, and preaching with the help of an interpreter. But he was so overpowering, so sure of himself, that the locals didn't trust him. Perhaps they thought that he was just another foreigner who didn't understand their ways and who probably had no sincere desire to know them or to understand them.

Although the Hong Kong residents were curious about him they fled from him in suspicion.

His Irish charm certainly didn't impress them. He was a foreigner with a foreign religion that people immediately dismissed. The reserved Chinese would bow politely and then, moving swiftly on silent feet, would disappear as quickly as they had come. The sincere but culturally naïve preacher was repeatedly left standing alone in the middle of a street that had been, only moments before, filled with people.

Robert couldn't understand what he was doing wrong. He smiled. He tried to look friendly. He held out his hand, and offered people tracts and Bibles. But they would all disappear. When he asked the interpreter why this was happening, the man just shrugged. His failure to reach the people began to affect Robert's spirit. His wife wasn't well enough to accompany him on these trips. She was suffering with her pregnancy and was unable to adjust to the heat. Aimee remained at home, still and calm, while Robert returned home each night, sad and despondent.

The Semples had brought less than $100 in savings with them, and the savings were almost gone. Other missionaries were in similar positions and simply had no funds to offer them. Robert realized that if the people refused to accept him, he and Aimee would have to go back to Canada. He kept his concerns from his 18-year-old wife. She had enough to worry about with the coming child. But Robert didn't want to admit defeat and return home.

Meanwhile Aimee longed for the comfort of a warm tub and a roaring fireplace. Even a cold glass of lemonade would have been wonderful. She was beginning to wonder if she knew this man who had taken her so far from her home. He didn't behave the way he had in Ingersoll. There, he was always strong and commanding but here, he was weak, uncertain, and tentative. It was as if he was waiting for something to happen.

Aimee never did like waiting. She usually had her feet planted firmly under her and she liked to move full speed ahead. But all the couple could do in this situation was to wait and to pray. Wait for an opening. Wait to be received. Wait while they learned the language of the people they were trying to help. Wait for patience. And wait for the baby who was due in three months.

And then, only a few weeks after their arrival, illness struck. Both the Semples contracted malaria. Aimee shivered with cold one minute and suffered with heat the next. She spent her days lying in the shade of the big trees in a nearby cemetery, crying out to God, and wondering if He had forsaken them.

Friends suggested they go to the Island of Macao, a few hours away, because the climate was milder there. But Aimee's health did not improve there. And Robert became even sicker than Aimee. They were forced to return to Hong Kong, where they were both admitted to a mission hospital for the poor.

Robert grew deathly ill and couldn't move from his bed. He developed dysentery, suffered unbearable thirst, and was constantly covered in sweat. Aimee managed to see him a few days after he was admitted. Robert was in another building, and the nurses had to almost carry her there. Aimee was adamant about being at his side. She had to see him and she was determined to make him well. Robert barely had the strength to speak and Aimee knew the instant she saw him that he was dying. With all her strength she cried out to God. But Robert calmly told her that his time had come. Robert Semple died of dysentery on August 17, 1910. He was 29 years old and they had just celebrated their second wedding anniversary.

On the very day that Robert died, a letter came to Aimee from two strangers in Chicago. They said that God had told them to send her money. There was $60 in the envelope, just enough to hold a funeral for Robert and to buy him a plot in Happy Valley Cemetery.

Aimee remained in the hospital until her daughter was born about a month after Robert's death. In deep sorrow, she named her Roberta. The baby was not at all well as she was also affected by malaria. Heartbroken, and convinced that she needed a healthy environment in which to raise her child, Aimee abandoned the mission in China. And with money wired to her by her mother — Aimee Semple set sail for San Francisco — desperate and alone.

Chapter 2
Escaping a Life of Domesticity

imee arrived in California in the winter of 1910. The passengers on the Empress of Ireland had collected $65 to help her get by train to New York where her mother was waiting.

Minnie Kennedy had abandoned the farm in Canada a few months before. She had set out for New York on her own to assist the thousands of immigrants pouring in from southern and eastern Europe, who were crowding the tenement houses in lower Manhattan. The Salvation Army had called out for help and Minnie responded with all the fervour and skills she possessed. Aimee's mother had a fine organizational mind and a hard-working practicality that created order and cleanliness wherever she went.

Minnie was in charge of fundraising for a large

downtown borough. She wore her black Salvation Army uniform proudly, with a broad bonnet and a large bow tied neatly underneath her neck. Minnie had a uniform ready for Aimee when she arrived. Aimee didn't argue. She embraced the Salvation Army to keep peace with her mother. And she knew that in service to others she might overcome her own sorrow.

Thus, Mother and daughter came together again in a bond of practicality. Never had the two been so united in purpose. Although Minnie was not entirely comfortable with whom Aimee was, she could at least approve of what she did for a while. This gave Aimee a much-needed sense of security in the midst of her suffering. At this difficult time she needed her mother desperately — and she was prepared to do anything to gain her approval — because she no longer felt the approval of God.

Aimee went to work for the Army right after she arrived. At night she collected money for the poor in the lobbies of the fashionable theatres on Broadway. And in the daytime, she served meals to the poor in midtown New York. She was happy to be of assistance. Keeping busy kept Aimee's mind off her grief and off her worry about her lingering illness and that of her child.

While she was collecting money for the Salvation Army in the theatre district, Aimee caught the eye of a 23-year-old restaurant cost accountant. Tall, muscular, Harold McPherson was the descendent of a family of Nova Scotia fishermen. He was used to working with his hands and thinking on his feet, and he liked Aimee's compassionate spirit and hard-working practicality. Harold began to walk Aimee home after her late shifts, sensing that she needed his protection. She liked having the presence of this big strong man. It didn't seem to bother Harold that she was still quite weak with malaria. He clearly wanted to take care of Aimee and her daughter, and Aimee began to lean on Harold more and more.

Minnie told Aimee that Harold was wrong for her. He was too "worldly." But it didn't take Harold long to win Aimee's heart. She was needy and he was there for her. But one thing haunted her. Would he understand? Could he cope if she was suddenly called back into the ministry? He assured her he would allow her to put God first.

So Aimee married Harold and became Aimee Semple McPherson. The young couple decided to settle in Chicago where there was a thriving Pentecostal Mission, which Aimee had visited with Robert just before they left for China. She knew she would be happy there. But Harold was not at all happy in Chicago. He wasn't comfortable in Pentecostal circles, and he didn't want his wife getting involved with these overly emotional people. Before long he suggested they go back to his home in Providence, Rhode Island, to live with his mother in her boarding house.

Aimee did not want to leave her Pentecostal friends, but she felt it was her duty to go with her husband. She knew the moment she arrived in Providence that she had made a mistake. Harold's mother wanted a dainty stay-at-home wife for Harold, one who would knit and crochet and tend the house. But Aimee longed to be out in the streets caring for the poor and spreading the gospel. One day, when her lot in life suddenly overcame her, Aimee collapsed into an easy chair and wept. She hadn't cried so hard since Robert died. At that moment, she realized that she had made a mistake in marrying Harold, but she didn't want to admit it, even to herself. Aimee was pregnant again. Rolf McPherson was born in March of 1913. Minnie promptly arrived to take care of the new baby, and to help Aimee and Harold find a home of their own, away from Harold's mother.

After Rolf was born Aimee got very sick. She had one operation after the other, first an appendectomy, then a hysterectomy. She developed massive internal bleeding but the doctors couldn't figure out where the bleeding was coming from. The surgeons kept opening her up, hoping to find the cause for her internal difficulties. But the source could not be found in her body, and Aimee would not accept any help for her mind. By 1914, the surgeons had taken out all the organs that they could, and still she bled. They told Aimee that unless she stopped bleeding, she was going to die.

Aimee would have welcomed death if it had taken her away from her domestic prison. She propped herself up on the pillows of her hospital bed, and cried out unto God. She heard a muffled voice answer her ... no ... it couldn't be ... or could it? At first she thought it was just the morphine. Her mind was foggy. Although many people she knew had heard the voice of God, she had a hard time believing that God would actually talk to her. After all, Aimee Semple McPherson was just an ordinary farm girl from Canada.

But there it was — the voice — saying, "Will you go? Now will you go?" It was clearer now. Yes. It had to be God. She was sure of it. "Now will you go?" What a strange thing for Him to say to her. Go where? She was too sick to get up on her feet. What could He possibly mean? But Aimee wasn't taking any chances, "Yes God. I'll go," was her meek and tentative response. She had no idea what He was talking about, but she was too weak to argue. "Yes I'll go," she said, a little more firmly. Then, she slowly began to realize what God meant. He wanted her to continue the work that she had begun with Robert in China, to win lost souls. That was it. She relaxed and lay back on her pillow.

Aimee was at peace for the first time in a very long while. Warmth filled her body and her being. She yawned and stretched. She could feel the blood circulating to her toes and she sat up by herself for the first time in days. She felt strangely alive. There were pins and needles all through her body … as if she had been asleep for a very long time. Reflecting on this, Aimee realized she had been asleep. Her spirit had been unable or unwilling to respond to the spirit of God within her. She attempted to stand up, but immediately fell down. She had been unable to walk for days.

The nurse came to her rescue and helped her get back

on the bed. Aimee told the startled nurse that God had healed her and that she was going home. The nurse called for a doctor. An elderly doctor entered and examined Aimee. The nurse told him that Aimee was delirious, that she was trying to leave the hospital. The doctor told the nurse that Aimee appeared stronger. Aimee emphatically told them that she was going home, that she had been healed. The doctor told her that he would call her husband.

When Harold arrived the next morning, Aimee was dressed and ready to go home. But she was not the needy sick wife he had come to claim. Aimee was a bright and bubbly woman who insisted that she was about to become an evangelist. Harold sat down on the bed, unable to absorb what Aimee was telling him. She said that God had told her to go out on the road and preach the gospel. Harold pointed out that he couldn't see how that would be possible when she had two small children and he had a job. Harold held his head in his hands. He had a headache. Aimee kept talking in a very loud and hysterical voice. Harold remained silent. He dared not interrupt or contradict her when she was in this hysterical state. He would have to wait until her excitement wore down before she would listen to him.

When Aimee calmed down, Harold told her firmly that she could not go on the road. He had a job and she had to care for the children. Harold told her she had to choose between him and God. It didn't take her long to decide what to do. Aimee was well aware that her father, now in his seventies, needed her help back on the farm in Ontario, and that he longed to see his grandchildren. Minnie had, by this time, returned to the farm and she had already offered to send Aimee the money for her escape. So, not long after her discharge from the hospital, Aimee packed up the children and headed for the train station while her husband was working the night shift.

Chapter 3
The Gift of Healing

S oon after arriving back in Canada in June 1915, Aimee attended a Pentecostal Camp Meeting in Berlin (now Kitchener, Ontario). She prayed for people to receive the baptism of the Holy Spirit as they knelt at the altar after each evening service. Aimee was so successful at "praying people through" to speaking in tongues that she began to receive invitations to preach in other towns. This posed no problem for Aimee, as her young son and daughter could remain on the farm under the watchful care of their grandmother.

Mount Forest, a small town in southwest Ontario, was the site of Aimee's first solo crusade. During the first few nights of meetings, her congregation consisted of a small number of people who had already been converted. But

Aimee wanted to win the lost and she wanted a full house. She remembered a tactic the Salvation Army used for bringing in the crowds, the "hallelujah run." She carried a wooden chair down to a corner of the main intersection in downtown Mount Forest, climbed on top of it, closed her eyes, and pointed her arms up to the sky. She froze like a statue and didn't move. She held the position, completely motionless, until she could hear people gathering around her. Young boys taunted her, trying to make her lose her concentration. They laughed and threw gum wrappers at her until their parents arrived and scolded them.

She could hear old women muttering and clicking their teeth and she smelled the aroma of pipe tobacco from the men who stood quietly gawking. She heard a grandfather clock strike the hour, but still she did not move. Her arms were beginning to ache and she prayed intently for God to ease her pain. In her flowing white dress, her waist-long hair piled up on top of her head, she resembled the motionless statue of a Greek goddess.

When she was sure that a large enough crowd had gathered, she yelled, "Follow me!" Then she ran as fast as she could back toward the mission. The crowd followed wondering what this crazed woman was going to do. There hadn't been this much excitement in downtown Mount Forest in years.

When she reached Victory Hall the crowd followed her in like rats lead by a pied piper — and once they were all inside — she slammed the door shut and locked it. She made no attempt to unlock the door again until she had finished speaking. But instead of complaining, the crowd was mesmerized. Aimee was entertaining. She was funny. She was colourful. This woman was a born storyteller, who could speak the language of the common people, and Aimee convinced people that God loved them. The next night the crowd was much bigger. They loved this positive style of preaching. Most of the evangelical Christians in southern Ontario were used to hearing about hellfire and damnation, and about a frightening vengeful God.

Aimee told them about a loving God who wanted to help them develop as human beings, and to help them find their full potential. She told them God wanted them to use their gifts and to be happy. Aimee sang rousing joyous hymns. And she made people laugh. They felt better when they left her services than they did when they came in.

Aimee had had no formal training in how to be a minister. She had only worked with her husband Robert for a few years, and he also had no formal training. She poured through the scriptures searching for ideas that would help her to become a better preacher. She took her examples for ministry from the lives of St. Paul and the apostle Peter. There was no flesh and blood minister to teach her and no role model to fashion herself after. She simply did what she felt God was asking her to do, and she gathered her ideas from prayer. Day after day, she was on her knees for hours seeking God's will, His voice, and His vision. She heard His voice clearly now every single day.

Aimee waited to hear the voice of God to tell her when to sing a hymn, when to pray, when to preach, and when to call out a prophecy (a premonition about something that was to occur in the future). She waited for a word of knowledge (a revelation about something she could not have ordinarily known). Aimee believed that every word she spoke during her services came directly from God and that she was under His anointing. She spoke with great conviction. And she never spoke unless she felt God was telling her to speak.

Her services kept getting longer and longer, with people continuing to pray late into the night. Many, including Aimee, would cross the street to go to the home of the mission's minister, Elizabeth Sharpe, after the service ended. Once there, Aimee guided them to receive the Holy Spirit.

Every night, the crowd grew. It would double the size of the night before. By the end of the first week of meetings, a crowd of 500 filled the vacant lot behind the church. Aimee realized she had to do something to keep her flock out of the rain. She decided to buy a large tent and, coincidentally, managed to find one in a nearby town. Although it was filled with holes and mildew, she managed to patch it together and raise it up.

Aimee knew by this time that being an evangelist and soul-winner was God's will for her. Although Harold had written her several letters begging her to come back to Rhode

Island, Aimee knew she could never go back. She sent him a telegram telling him that the two of them might be happy if he would go "her way" into full-time evangelism. She didn't receive a response.

One night, a disabled man walked to the front of her tent while she was conducting a meeting. The man was well known in the community because of his deformity, a crippled leg with running sores. He was the town bell ringer, the one who rang out the noon and supper hours and who called people to meetings. He asked Aimee to pray that God would heal him. Aimee felt her heart leap into her throat. She stepped forward in faith — put her hands on his leg — and asked God to heal him. She didn't really expect the man to be healed, but she hoped that he would, even though, to her knowledge, no congregants had ever been healed before when she prayed over them.

Aimee's hands became hot. Sweat dripped off her brow. She filled a cloth with anointed oil and wrapped it around his sores. Heat began to flow into her hands. Aimee quietly prayed, with all the faith she could muster, that a miracle would happen to this man. She asked the congregation to pray with her. Then she waited for God to make a move. Nothing happened. A few minutes later, the man quietly limped out of the building and into the street. And she led the congregation in a rousing hymn to cover her disappointment.

The Gift of Healing

Love lifted me
When nothing else could help
Love lifted me.

A few days later, the man returned. Aimee opened up the cloth on his leg in front of the congregation and was amazed to see that the running sores were gone. He had been completely and miraculously healed. The crowd cheered. Aimee Semple McPherson's healing ministry had begun. Delirious with joy, the bell ringer ran out into the streets shouting and showing people what God had done. And Aimee knew that her life and her ministry would never be the same from that moment on.

People began to flock around her, asking to be prayed over for a physical healing. She was overwhelmed by the requests for physical restoration. Her reputation grew like wildfire. The message was spreading far and wide. Even those who had never been to her meetings requested healing prayers. People came to her from all of the Christian denominations. Everyone in her services was treated the same no matter what background they came from or what church they went to. She told the congregation that the love of God made them all one. She refused to take sides with any particular denomination, preferring to stress the Pentecostal "experience" over the Pentecostal denomination.

Her messages were about empowerment, the empowerment of women ... of ethnic and racial minorities ... and of the uneducated, the poor, and the sick. Where other preachers might have shunned the bell ringer, Aimee had embraced him and all that he represented. He was her bridge into another world, the world of the sick and needy, and that was the arena where she felt she was meant to do her greatest work.

Aimee Semple McPherson tried to meet the needs of anyone who came to her. If she had extra food she fed people. If she had extra clothes she gave them away. If someone needed money and she had it, she was generous. She didn't just give to Christians who thought the way she did, she gave to all.

Sometimes the Mount Forest congregation sang for hours at the close of the service, going deeper and deeper into the presence of God. Sometimes Aimee could barely look up. She was taken so deep into the heart of God that she could barely move. The air was so thick with His presence that she felt as if she were walking through thick fog. Everything seemed to happen in slow motion and she was guided directly by the hand of God. She could feel God's hand nudging her back, pushing in this direction or that, gently guiding her. God was telling her what to say and what to do, whom to pray with, and for how long.

Then one day, into the midst of one of her services walked Harold McPherson. He stood in front of Aimee, watching her work. To her great astonishment he reverently knelt at the altar. He asked that she pray over him so he could receive the baptism in the Holy Spirit. Aimee knelt beside him. Others laid their hands on him as well. Aimee sensed sincerity in this simple man, her husband, and perhaps he showed a little more openness and conviction. It wasn't many minutes before he began to speak in other tongues. Should she trust him? Was he just pretending to be baptized in the Holy Ghost so that she would return with him to Rhode Island?

Later that night Harold confessed to Aimee that he had come to take her back, kicking and screaming if necessary, but when he heard her preach something had come over him and made him change his mind. He had never heard preaching like that before. He told her it touched his heart and that he knew he couldn't restrain her. He knew that he must support her in God's work. He promised Aimee that if she came back to Rhode Island with him, he would go on the road with her as an evangelist. Aimee decided that she had to give him another chance.

The two travelled back to the farm to tell Aimee's parents. Over Minnie's protests, Aimee made preparations to leave. Minnie was sure that Aimee was doing the wrong thing. Minnie said that under no circumstances would she allow Roberta to go with Aimee on the road preaching. After all, the four-year old child was still sick from the effects of the malaria she had been exposed to in the Far East. Roberta must remain on the farm. So Aimee packed up two-year-old Rolf, and left Roberta in the continuing care of her grandmother. This was not a hardship for little Roberta as she and her grandmother were very close. Aimee and Harold left with their son to expand Aimee's ministry into the United States.

Chapter 4
The Revivalist Road

When the McPhersons returned to Rhode Island, true to his word, Harold quit his job, sold their belongings, and bought a tent big enough to hold a large crowd. But he was uncomfortable with the idea of accepting charity in order to pay for their basic living expenses. No one in his family had ever gone without a job. He felt it was demeaning to accept handouts from strangers just because he and his wife were going out to preach.

Aimee, on the other hand, had no problem allowing God to supply her needs nor in accepting handouts. She and her first husband had prayed for food, money, clothing, housing, and transportation and it had always come in, even the money for a funeral for Robert had miraculously appeared at exactly the right time.

However, shortly before they were about to launch their first revival crusade, Harold found work. Aimee left for the revival meeting in Providence alone. She was every bit as popular there as she had been in Mount Forest. Every night the crowd got bigger. More and more people were baptized in the Holy Ghost and were being healed by Aimee.

With a successful campaign in Providence behind her, Aimee moved on to Massachusetts, to the Pentecostal Montwait Camp meeting where she was booked to preach for the summer, along with several other prominent Pentecostal preachers. Her peers were beginning to recognize her. She knew that it was unusual for a woman to receive this kind of recognition, as only a few women evangelists had dared to travel throughout the United States holding crusades on their own. The stories of miraculous healings in her meetings had spread throughout Pentecostal circles. This was all the more impressive because there were very few evangelists, of either sex, who had physical healings taking place in their meetings.

Aimee had several types of physical healings occurring. She had blind people whose sight was restored, deaf people who regained their hearing, and people, who had one leg longer than the other, whose shorter limb grew. Men who had industrial injuries had their mangled arms straighten out. Every kind of illness imaginable was being healed when Aimee prayed over people.

Although Aimee emphatically stated that the healings were the result of God's power and that they didn't have anything to do with her personally, many people thought they did. Sick people flocked around her, truly believing that she was the source of the cures. Sceptics began to call her a "hypnotist" who compelled people to let go of their fears, thus creating a positive attitude in which healing would naturally take place. Many were convinced it was Aimee's enthusiasm and hope that resulted in healing.

Talk like this frightened Aimee. She called herself "Little Aimee, a simple farm girl." How could anyone possibly think that she was a professional hypnotist? She had no training in how to manipulate people. Surely the public must realize that the healings resulted from the power of God working through her. She knew she couldn't heal anyone on her own.

News of Aimee's outstanding popularity and success reached Harold. The truth was he wasn't all that thrilled with his job, and it sounded like she was having a whole lot more fun than he was. Besides, he missed his son Rolf. One night after a service ended, a startled Aimee looked up and saw Harold standing at the back of the church. He moved slowly towards her carrying suitcases. As they left the large tent, Harold told her that he'd been having dreams every night telling him to join her in the ministry. He claimed that he had quit his job and had come to stay. Aimee took him to the small tent where she slept and they talked late into the night. She told him he was welcome to travel with her, but only if he surrendered his heart completely to God. He swore to her that he would and she decided, once again, to give him another chance.

Her time at Montwait was almost over and Aimee had no idea where she was supposed to go next. She asked Harold to pray diligently that God would give her an answer. She had offers of places to go and preach, but she would not go anywhere until she heard directly from God. She didn't always get a clear message from God, and for several days she had heard Him say the word "Corona." Corona? She had never heard of a church, or a place, or even a person called Corona.

Within a few days she received a letter from a woman in Queen's inviting her to come and launch a revival in her district of New York City, a district called Corona. Aimee knew in an instant that this was where she was supposed to go. Harold reluctantly agreed to take her. When the McPhersons arrived at the woman's apartment, they found out that she had not made any preparations for their meetings. There was no hall. No money. Not even any supporters to help set things up. Aimee decided to try to persuade one of the local ministers to let her use his church. Eventually, she located the minister of a Swedish Baptist Church who was willing to let her use his sanctuary for midweek meetings. She started small, but as in Mount Forest, the crowds grew quickly. Soon Aimee found a church with a larger sanctuary under the Free Gospel banner. And there she remained for several weeks, until she collected enough money to move on to Florida where, she was sure, God was telling her to go next. All the while Aimee was gaining confidence and the crowds were gaining confidence in her.

It took several weeks to drive down to Florida. Many of the roads were impassable and the car kept getting stuck in the mud. Aimee was glad that she had Harold to help her lug the car out of the mud holes and to fix the tires that went flat several times a day. On the way across the country they fished and ate berries and apples off the trees. Aimee spread the gospel wherever she went, never missing an opportunity to share her faith with anyone that happened by. Harold often wondered if she was capable of talking about any other topic. He swore she preached in her sleep. He could see her clenching her teeth and muttering and shaking.

Aimee was aware that Harold got agitated whenever she tried to win someone's soul. He preferred her to be low key, letting people see her way of life and ask her about her faith. But she couldn't hold it in and found herself shouting, "Jesus saves! Jesus saves!" She even painted a gospel message on the side of their car in big bold letters, and made up tracts to hand out to the people they met. The word had to get out. It just had to. Aimee was excited, as excited as she had been when she first met Robert. Her life was changing for the better. She was moving forward into eternity — into glory — and she wanted to take everyone she could with her.

Harold enjoyed the trip. It was a relaxing vacation, and he loved being away from the pressures of his regular job. But he couldn't imagine living like this for an extended period of time. He liked to have an easy to chair relax in, a warm cup of tea, and a fire in the fireplace to cosy up to. He always felt damp on the road and he never got a good sleep in the back seat of a car or on the ground in a tent. He wanted to sleep in a real bed. Nothing seemed to bother his wife. She took it all in stride, just happy to be doing God's work. Harold thought that, just once, if he could actually hear the voice of God then he wouldn't be so critical of his wife. He really wanted to enter the same state of lunacy that possessed Aimee. It seemed to protect her from feeling any kind of earthly discomfort. She inhabited a spiritual realm where nothing else seemed to matter. His wife's number one joy in life was listening to the voice of God — and it didn't matter what God said — she followed it to the letter. How could Harold question it when he couldn't hear it?

He began to think it was possible that she had come up with an ingenious method of getting her own way. Perhaps, whatever thought entered her head was what she did, and she expected him to follow. But Aimee fervently believed the voice was God's and there was no arguing with her. She told Harold that God's voice was music in her ears, and that it was the rhythm in which she moved and breathed and danced. She couldn't imagine living without it. It connected her to life, to energy, to vision and she knew that if she heard God's voice and obeyed it, she could never go wrong. Somehow, everything would turn out all right. "All things work together for good for them that love the Lord," she would quote to Harold, from the Bible.

Aimee and Harold finally arrived in Jacksonville,

Florida, several weeks after they had left the northeast. Aimee just knew wonderful things were about to happen. She could feel God's presence in the campground where she was about to hold her crusade. She went out and prayed for God to consecrate the grounds. Harold interrupted to remind her that that they had no dinner. Their son was hungry, but there was no nearby lake with fish nor were there any trees with fruit. Harold reminded his wife that they didn't have a dime between them.

Aimee began to pray. A few minutes later a prepaid shipment of clothing and food arrived from her supporters in Corona. Instead of getting excited, Harold got really angry. This type of occurrence was going to cause his wife to go deeper and deeper into a dream world where she would expect anything they needed to magically appear. This was a coincidence, not a miracle, he told her. How could he convince her to consider the needs of their child, to think about the safety of her family, or to work reasonable hours? How could he convince her to talk to him about something — anything — other than God?

Harold was a Christian, but he had been raised to believe that God helps those that help themselves. It was his job to provide for his family, not God's. God expected him to work long and hard and not just to sit back and pray and wait for their food and clothing. Harold watched in dismay as his highly excitable wife tore open the parcels of clothing and made hysterical squeals over each new dress. Their son was enthusiastically exploring the food, while Harold sat back from a distance refusing to take part in the revelry. This was not a miracle. This was charity. And he was above that. He left the tent to take a walk. The trees were wet after a damp rain and everything looked so fresh and new. He breathed deeply and thanked God for the gift of life. But he wished he was anywhere but where he was.

In the church where Harold was raised, when people became missionaries, their church body sponsored them. They didn't just go out on their own and expect miracles from God to meet their everyday needs. But he had to admit that it wasn't the charitable dependency that angered him the most. It was the feeling that he was in competition with God for his wife's attention. Harold had gradually begun to realize that Aimee would never depend on him the way she depended on God. Harold also realized that he was not a good preacher like his wife. In fact, he was far from it. His personality and temperament were more suited to accounting than public speaking. He worked hard to prepare a good sermon. He studied the lectionaries and scriptures. He prayed. He consulted other believers. But when it came time to get up and speak, he just didn't have the gusto or the sense of humour that his wife had. He couldn't hold the crowd's attention and he had no idea how to tell a story so that folks would end up laughing at themselves. And he definitely couldn't translate the Bible into everyday language the way Aimee could. Furthermore, Harold was not comfortable with a whole lot of noise and activity. His God lived in silence most of the time, preferring that people use their minds, not the wild emotions that Aimee evoked. Harold wasn't sure if he would ever get used to the extreme emotionalism of revival meetings. To him, it had nothing to do with faith.

Harold looked after their two-year-old son while Aimee went off to prepare her sermons. He tried not to be angry with her; it wasn't her fault that the food and clothing had arrived. Nor was it her fault that she was a better speaker than he was. He tried to tell himself to be patient, but his patience was wearing thin. He was getting tired of being the babysitter and tired of being the minister's husband.

The crowds increasingly adored Aimee. More and more miracles were occurring in her ministry. Desperate people pressed in to spend time with her. She never had time to spend with Harold and Rolf. Harold desperately wanted to stop feeling like God's second best. Nevertheless, he stayed on the road with Aimee for a year-and-a-half. They travelled up and down the eastern seaboard spending summer in the north and winter in the south. Harold pitched tents, built altars, carried pianos, connected the electricity, and even cleared the grounds. But all the while, he believed he was meant to be more than an amateur carpenter and a babysitter. In the midst of a long crusade in Key West, he left for Providence. Alone.

Aimee's Key West crusade went on uninterrupted. She couldn't let the crowds know that anything was wrong. She sang at the top of her lungs and worked late into the night. She didn't let on to anyone that she was angry. But she was angry, angrier than she had ever been in her entire life. She had given God what he wanted. Why did He allow her husband to abandon the cause? It was hard to run the crusades alone.

The truth of the matter was that Aimee still missed Robert terribly. She always felt that he was with her, up there with God, praying for her and cheering her on because she was carrying on the work that God had called them both to do. She routinely put his photograph up in a place of prominence wherever she went. Over and over, she begged Robert's forgiveness for marrying Harold. In reality, she couldn't forgive herself. Fortunately, when she concentrated on preaching and praying with total devotion she was able to forget her mistakes, at least for a while.

Her problems and insecurities, however, always emerged when she tried to sleep. Although she had enough energy to sustain her through the day, she couldn't let go enough at night to get a proper rest. She was always excited, always exuberant, always giving her all. Aimee found herself praying late into the night, often falling asleep for brief moments on her knees. But as soon as she lay back in her bed, she tossed and turned all night long.

So after Harold left and after many sleepless nights, Aimee did what she always did when she was in over her head. She wired her mother for help. And Minnie came. For one thing, Minnie wanted to find out if the letters Aimee was sending her were really true. Were people's arthritic bodies really straightening out? Was her daughter drawing crowds as large as 1500? Were the coloureds and the whites worshipping together in the same church? She found it impossible to believe. Yet, she had never known Aimee to be a liar.

In March 1918, Minnie and her granddaughter Roberta arrived in Key West and soon saw that everything Aimee had told them was true. The crowds were even larger than Aimee had described, and many individuals were being miraculously healed every night. Minnie's eyes bulged out of their sockets.

In no time at all, Aimee was listening to Minnie's advice almost as often as she listened to God's. Where Harold McPherson had failed to gain influence over Aimee, Minnie adeptly gained control.

Chapter 5
Mother Knows Best

S oon after Minnie arrived in Florida she began to organize Aimee's ministry. At first Aimee resented Minnie's heavy-handedness, but then she realized that Minnie was doing a much better job than she had done at managing things.

Minnie wrote hundreds of letters to churches and religious organizations all over North America emphasizing Aimee's speaking ability and healing gifts, and advising them of her availability. She astutely realized that publicity would be the key to Aimee's success, and she set about getting her daughter's name in print. Minnie began to transform the small monthly newsletter that Aimee had originated, *The Bridal Call*, into a 16-page publication, complete with pictures, sermons, and testimonials. She initiated a subscription price of 25 cents annually. Minnie became an accomplished photographer by taking dozens of photographs of Aimee. There were family photos with the children, dramatic pictures of her preaching, and soft images of Aimee in fashionable dresses with flowers. Minnie brilliantly created an image of her daughter as a pure, gentle, pious woman dedicated to doing God's work.

During this time, Minnie hired a stenographer so that Aimee's stories and ideas would always be recorded. Too often the evangelist's most insightful visions and witty commentary had been lost because Aimee was preaching and her mother was helping to control the crowds. Minnie realized that someone had to be taking notes down at all times so that these valuable pronouncements and insights would be preserved. The stenographer often typed well into the night writing up her notes and preparing manuscripts and sermons for the overburdened evangelist.

Thanks to Minnie's talent for publicity, Aimee began to receive offers to preach all over North America. Minnie insisted on advance fees to cover their travelling expenses before making a booking. Aimee thought asking for money up front was a little pushy. She asked her mother to be more flexible, explaining that not everyone had the money to send in advance. She pointed out that it might be God's will for her to go somewhere where people could not afford to pay. But Minnie insisted that only those who could pay the expense would hear Aimee preach. They were no longer going to head out with nothing in their pockets hoping to find a cloud with a silver lining. The practical Minnie also insisted on collecting and keeping track of all of the money that came in and went out. Aimee didn't argue.

The astute business manager also asked anyone wanting to book Aimee for meetings to find them a rent-free vacant lot where they could pitch their tent or, alternately, to find them a suitable building to rent. She also insisted that they locate a piano and round up some volunteer workers in advance of the arrival of Aimee's entourage. Minnie decided to book Aimee for revival meetings of one to four weeks in duration, leaving lots of time in between engagements in case Aimee was asked to stay longer than expected. Minnie realized that once people began to be healed in large numbers, it was going to be hard for her daughter to get away.

Minnie had taken her time sorting things out in Key West before pushing Aimee forward. She knew that her daughter needed time to recover from Harold's departure, even if she was reluctant to talk about it. Aimee told her mother that she would love to head west, as she had already spent several years travelling up and down the eastern seaboard. She had heard wonderful stories about California and Colorado where there was a great migration underway. Aimee wanted to be part of it, and Minnie decided that she'd like to see a little more of the country herself.

Aimee was really enjoying her extended time in Key West. By taking over the business and administrative side of the ministry, Minnie had made it possible for Aimee to spend more time with her children. Aimee loved laughing, joking, and playing with Roberta and Rolf and telling them stories while strolling through the everglades. She was overjoyed that her daughter had joined her after more than three years apart. Roberta was now seven-and-a-half and she couldn't have been more like her father. The child listened attentively and could make intelligent conversation with anyone. She was patient, kind, and gentle with older people. Roberta was a child with a conscience who could tell the difference between right and wrong. Minnie had trained her well in how to be responsible, dutiful, and giving.

It didn't take long before Minnie told Aimee to stop spoiling the child. She was ruining everything Minnie had done with her. But Aimee couldn't help herself. She had been separated from her daughter for so long that she could not stop doting on Roberta and, as Minnie pointed out, favouring her. Aimee was so proud of Roberta, and she had never had the chance to show what a good mother she could be. The arrival of her daughter had given Aimee an excuse to pray a little less and play a little more. Although Aimee thought her mother was too structured and too controlling, she was tired of doing all of the work herself. And she had to admit that her mother was the more practical person.

After spending the summer holding revival meetings in Philadelphia, Aimee went to New York in the fall with her stenographer and family in tow. There was nothing that could have prepared her for the terrible scene that filled the streets. By October 1918, an average of 200 people per day were dying of the Spanish flu. There were not enough coffins to bury them all and the air was filled with the stench of decaying bodies. There was an overall sense of immense desperation.

It didn't take long for Aimee to get sick, but she still managed to preach with a fever and the chills. Roberta, who was always susceptible, got double pneumonia as a complication of the flu. In her deliria the child begged her mother for a permanent home where she would be warm and comfortable. She cried that didn't want to be dragged from place to place every few weeks. Aimee promised the child that she would have a home. A short time later, Aimee heard the voice of God telling her that He would raise her child, and give her "a little home in Los Angeles." Aimee began to picture it in her mind, a lovely little house surrounded by palm trees on a calm peaceful street where her vulnerable child would be safe from harm.

Meanwhile, the sick and desperate kept pounding on her door. How could she make them understand that she didn't have the power to heal them? Aimee didn't know why so many people were being healed at her meetings, but she continued to believe that it had nothing to do with her personally. It was totally up to God. Anyone could be healed if they asked God to heal them. All they had to do was pray. But still, the sick followed her everywhere. They believed she was their last hope. The doctors could not heal this flu. Many health care workers, who tried to assist the sick, ended up contracting the illness themselves. Many of them died.

Aimee decided that it might be very effective to dress as a warrior in the Lord's army against sickness and disease. She bought a series of white dresses that resembled the uniforms worn by battle nurses in the trenches of France. Every time she preached she wore one of these white uniforms and, for dramatic effect, threw a dark-coloured cape over her shoulders. Aimee was determined to demonstrate that she was in the army of the Lord, and that He was going to be victorious in this battle against the dark forces.

Just after the end of World War l, with her daughter miraculously restored to full health, Aimee began a cross-country trek. She dressed in her white uniform as though prepared to fight a battle. Around this time Aimee purchased a sturdy new Oldsmobile, knowing this was a car her family would be comfortable in. The family intended to spend all day every day for weeks on end travelling the countryside. At night they would have the large and comfortable Oldsmobile to sleep in. This car was going to be home. Aimee decided that she would be the only driver in a trip that would cover thousands of miles. It would be an adventure, and if there was one thing that Aimee loved, it was to experience new things. The United States was an uncharted wilderness waiting to be explored.

Aimee loved the backcountry, but her greatest challenge was the condition of the roads. Although cars had improved in recent years, the roads that criss-crossed the United States

Canadian-born evangelist Aimee Semple McPherson,
shown in 1918 with her "gospel car."

had not. They were little more than cattle trails with wagon ruts. Fallen trees or stubborn livestock often blocked the road. Car tires blew often and Aimee became good at changing tires. Still, she was cautious. They travelled behind other vehicles, whenever possible, in case anything happened to the car. They carried large cans of gasoline and of water, and averaged 200 kilometres a day. It's possible that Aimee may have been among the first women to drive across the United States without a man.

Minnie, the stenographer, and Aimee slept in the back of the car while the children slept on a cot stretched out between the front and back seats. Although most of the roads were not well travelled during this period, there was no need to worry about predators. The travellers were alone most of the time. The cross-country trip provided Aimee, for at least several hours each day, with a break in her relentless schedule. She began to feel free — like an ordinary citizen with time on her hands — even if most of it was spent at the wheel. Aimee loved the trip. This was a precious time with the children and she took advantage of every moment of it. She pointed out birds and animals and trees along the way, making every mile a learning experience for them. Even Minnie had to admit she was enjoying herself. And Aimee had never been happier.

Every time they stopped, Aimee would hand out spiritual tracts and talk to anyone who would listen about God. She prayed over the sick and stopped to preach at small revival meetings along the way. Churches were closed in an attempt to prevent spreading the still virulent flu. But, miraculously, every time Aimee approached a town, the ban had been lifted just before she arrived. Public meetings were suddenly allowed. And often, the ban would be back in place just as soon as the small group left.

By the time Aimee arrived in California in the middle of December 1918, the flu epidemic was beginning to wane. She had only one day to prepare for revival meetings that were already booked in the downtown Pentecostal Victory Hall. She handed the children over to Minnie and went to work. There were sermons to prepare.

Her first few meetings brought in a good crowd. Stories of her miraculous healings had spread across the land, and there had never been a time in U.S. history when people had been more desperate to experience healing. By the end of the first week of meetings, the crowd was overflowing the 1000-seat auditorium. Subsequently, Minnie managed to book the 3500-seat Temple Auditorium. Aimee kept it filled for more than two months.

One night a woman announced to the congregation that the Lord had instructed her to give Aimee a lot on which to build a house. One after the other, people spoke up and offered their gifts: masonry, bricklaying, roofing, carpentry, even furniture-making and landscaping. The vision Aimee had had of a little house was finally coming to fruition. Aimee stood in awe at what was unfolding in front of her eyes. It took just three months for the completion of the house. Aimee hired a housekeeper to care for the children while she and Minnie travelled. In April 1919, just four months after they arrived in the west, they headed east again to Tulsa, Oklahoma. By June they were in Chicago and by July they had arrived in New York City, where Minnie took scores of photographs and screened Aimee's articles for their monthly newsletter.

Although Aimee had opposed many of her mother's changes to the structure of her ministry at first, she had begun to realize that her mother was making things easier for her, freeing her from having to do menial tasks for which she was ill-equipped. Her mother always had her schedule prepared by the time they arrived somewhere new, as well as a warm meal and a cup of milk. Aimee had never been more productive, she was writing sermons, dictating articles, and praying over more and more people every day. She even managed to publish her autobiography.

Aimee had always been able to hold the crowd's attention with humour and dramatic storytelling. But since the Spanish flu epidemic, people didn't want to listen to a sermon. They wanted to be prayed over by Aimee alone. But it was impossible for one person to pray over more than 1000 people, individually, at every meeting. Soon after they reached Baltimore in December 1919 — Aimee went down into the basement of the Lyric Theatre — and wept. She simply could not cope with the increasing demands that were being made on her.

Minnie's reaction to Aimee's dilemma was to figure out a way to give the crowd what they wanted using the most efficient means possible. She decided to develop the most effective method of conducting a healing crusade that the world had ever seen. Minnie began to train volunteers, just days before the crusades started, in how to care for the sick, how to usher people through buildings, and how to control crowds.

On the day of each revival meeting, Minnie would

arrive at the meeting place hours before Aimee did, and she instructed the invalids to arrive early as well. A section of the hall, near the front, was roped off for the sick and they were allowed in hours before the general public was admitted. Minnie asked the volunteers to interview those who required prayers for healing, and to assist each one to fill out a prayer card with their name, address, faith affiliation, and a description of their disease or affliction. All the cards were numbered so that they could be called up for prayer in an orderly fashion. When the time came for Aimee to pray over the sick, Minnie would place a number on the blackboard at the front of the hall. When a person's number was placed on the board they would be ushered forward for prayer.

Minnie arranged for seven chairs to be placed horizontally across the front of the auditorium, with their backs to the congregation. Minnie insisted on chairs, because in previous meetings many had fallen over backwards in a swoon after Aimee prayed over them, thus crushing the invalids behind them. Minnie's motto was "protect Aimee," and she did. She stood beside her on the platform co-ordinating the people who came forward for prayer, while holding the vessel of healing oil for Aimee. Minnie also made sure that any healings that took place were recorded. At the altar, Minnie worked as hard, if not harder, than Aimee. And her sharp eyes didn't miss a second of what was going on.

During a healing service in Washington, D.C., at McKendree Methodist Episcopal Church, a young man walked up the aisle towards Aimee and asked her to anoint his handkerchief with healing oil. He tearfully told the congregation that his mother had been thrown from a streetcar and was in a cast from her neck down. And, he said, tuberculosis had taken over her spine and the doctors had no cure for it. Aimee filled the cloth with oil, prayed over it, and told the man to place the cloth underneath his mother's cast, and expect God's best.

A few days later, a woman named Mrs. Jackson came walking slowly up the aisle towards the platform with a man supporting her arm. He explained to Aimee that he was the woman's doctor, and that he had been treating her since she had been thrown from the streetcar months before. He told Aimee that Mrs. Jackson had insisted that he remove her body cast. The doctor then stunned everyone by testifying that she had been healed after Aimee's prayer cloth had been placed underneath her cast. When he removed the cast, he explained, he discovered that Mrs. Jackson's body had been completely restored. Minnie immediately seized upon the opportunity. She insisted that the story of Mrs. Jackson's healing be included in *The Bridal Call*. This was Aimee's first medically documented healing.

The secular press "discovered" Aimee because of Mrs. Jackson. Many reporters didn't put much stock in faith healing because they believed that the so-called illnesses might have originated in people's minds. But Mrs. Jackson's healing was outstanding because it was medically documented. Here was a doctor who had confessed to having been a sceptic, who was now overwhelmed by what had just happened to his patient. Here was a man who thought like many of the reporters. He was a logical scientific thinker who believed that a miracle had just taken place. The press began to scrutinize Aimee's ministry and they soon realized that she was no run-of-the-mill revivalist. Aimee Semple McPherson was news.

Aimee welcomed the press as she would any other member of her congregation. She invited them, with their cameras and notepads, into her inner sanctum and after-hour prayer services, explaining patiently to them how the various gifts of the spirit manifested themselves. She became a translator of spiritual realities for the secular realm, not only in her sermons from the pulpit, or in the numerous articles she wrote, but also for the press, who came by the hundreds.

Aimee loved to take complex ideas and turn them into simple concepts. She was the master of the parable, the "illustrated sermon." She loved to act out the Bible stories in an enthusiastic and animated style, so that people who couldn't speak English very well could still understand. If Aimee told a Biblical parable about a wise virgin who always kept oil in her lamp, she would dress up in a toga and fill an old lamp with oil.

There was nothing about Aimee that the reporters couldn't understand. They called her innocent, vulnerable, even childlike. The aspect of Aimee's personality that the press appreciated the most was her positive attitude. They loved the uplifting tone of Aimee's messages. As a result, they liberally and regularly poked fun at fundamentalist preachers who screamed about hellfire and damnation, and angrily pounded the pulpit. But Aimee charmed them all with her quiet picture of a community of Christian love, generosity, and kindness. And the press particularly appreciated her sense of humour. Aimee poked fun at everything and everyone, even herself. Hellfire and damnation were seldom mentioned in Aimee's campaign. She talked about "justice" and "compassion" and "mercy" and most of all about the "love" of God. People from all walks of life felt comfortable in Aimee's meetings. People of all different colours and nationalities were made to feel welcome, as though they were part of a family.

Aimee radiated joy as she sashayed up and down the aisles singing and waving handkerchiefs.

It is joy unspeakable and full of glory
Full of glory, full of glory
It is joy unspeakable and full of glory
And the half has never yet been told.

Aimee made church fun. Even Minnie had to admit she was enjoying herself. The atmosphere of the nightly services was that of a large party where the guests were relaxed and felt at home. Even though they were large, Aimee's revival meetings turned into intimate gatherings of people who liked each other. Aimee kept the music flowing and the rhythm beating. She played the piano, selected the music, and led the songs, which were often hymns she had composed herself to suit special occasions.

Although most evangelists who had gone before her preferred to put "worship leaders" in charge of the music, Aimee realized what a valuable role in the service the music played. She preferred to lead the singing herself and chose hymns that made people stand up and take charge. In her nurse's uniform, she stormed the barracks of the elusive enemy of negativity and banished it with positive thinking, joyful music, and powerful passages of scripture that spoke of God's eternal love and concern for all His children. Aimee propagated a "gospel of joy."

Minnie stood on the platform right beside Aimee and sang. She could sing louder than the deepest booming bass. Even if Aimee stopped singing to call out a healing that was occurring spontaneously in the crowd, Minnie never missed a note. Minnie often set the mood and tone for the meetings. She told the musicians when to be silent and when to play a graceful melody underneath Aimee's sermon, thus creating a calming receptive atmosphere for healing. She could also rev up the volume when she felt the situation required it, much as she had done when she conducted the Salvation Army's brass bands on the street corners of southern Ontario 20 years before.

Minnie believed that many of the so-called works of the spirit, such as laughing in the spirit, dancing in the spirit, and some of the prophetic utterances were, perhaps — humanly inspired — and not divine. She put her foot down about the excess emotionalism at Aimee's meetings. She was concerned that mainstream Christians might run, because of the over-abundance of exuberance and strange spiritual manifestations that were occurring. Aimee understood her mother's concern. She realized the crowds were getting a little out of control. She decided to comply with Minnie's request and she began discouraging people who stood up to prophesy if she felt they were creating disorder and confusion in the meeting. If the offending party grew obnoxious, Aimee would immediately signal one of her assistants to usher them out.

Minnie took note of the fact that ministers and professionals from mainstream Protestant denominations were beginning to attend Aimee's services. By the end of 1920, Aimee had been offered Methodist credentials, and was celebrated in a national Methodist magazine. Later, the Baptists made her a similar offer, which she accepted. The Assemblies of God protested and she eventually returned her Pentecostal credentials to Springfield, Missouri. By this time, Aimee was adamant in her belief that she should not identify with one Christian denomination over another. But she often wondered what Robert, who had never left the Pentecostal fold, would have thought about this.

The crowds grew in overwhelming proportions now

that mainline Protestants were beginning to attend Aimee's meetings. Minnie was aware that she was soon going to have to take lessons in crowd control.

This issue came to a head when Aimee attempted to reach the 3000-seat Memorial Hall in Dayton, Ohio, in 1920. The street was blocked with people and Aimee's car was stopped two full blocks before her destination. There were people everywhere; some on foot, some carrying stretchers, some in wheel chairs, all scurrying in the same direction. The scene reminded her of Hong Kong in her last days with Robert. The streets were a sea of human bodies moving slowly forward carrying their burdens. The sick recognized Aimee and pressed their hands against the windows of her car. "Please pray for my sister! ... Please pray for my mother! ... Please! Please!" Aimee tried to shut them out. She closed her eyes, but more kept coming, pressing in closer and closer. It was a terrifying experience.

Police officers arrived frantically blowing their whistles. The crowd refused to disperse. There was nowhere for them to go because the street was completely jammed. Shots were fired into the air. Minnie got out of the car to help the police to direct traffic. The car was rocking side to side with the vibration of bodies pressing in against the car. Aimee closed her eyes again and struggled to breathe. Finally, the police formed a line from the car to the auditorium and motioned the driver to drive the car forward. The car slowly made its way to the side entrance of the hall. The building was already filled to capacity and more were fighting to get inside. In mass hysteria people were climbing through the windows — lowering themselves down from the roof — climbing onto the fire escape. The police physically pulled Aimee out of her seat and propelled her forward toward the door.

The door suddenly opened, just long enough for the officers to push Aimee through the narrow entrance and past the mirage of desperate faces. The heavy door slammed shut behind her. But in front of her, invalids jammed into every available space including the corridor, the stairwell, and the hallway. They were begging her to pray over them. She heard a noise like the roar of the ocean crashing against her ears. She pressed her hands tight over her ears but still she could hear the noise. The last thing she saw before she blacked out was a sea of wild and anguished faces. Aimee crumpled to the floor.

Chapter 6
Money from Heaven and Other Unusual Sources

his was a turning point in Aimee's career. Aimee longed to escape from the frightening crowds. She was suffering from exhaustion so deep that she had no idea what to do next. Her voice was worn out from the abuse it suffered in order for her to be heard in large auditoriums. At that time, there was no audio system adequate to amplify the human voice for the size of crowds her meetings drew. To make matters worse, Aimee was still not sleeping properly. She was desperate to find more time for herself, and especially more time to spend with her growing children.

Aimee had promised her daughter a house and a real home, but Aimee was never there. What good was it to give the child a home if her mother was not there? Her child was growing up without her. She had to find a way to preach and stay home at the same time. There was really only one solution. Aimee decided she would have to build a church near where she lived. But how could she build such a church? She didn't have the money that an enormous enterprise like this would need. Aimee had never taken up an offering, never passed the plate like other preachers did. She just asked for her basic expenses to be met and people gave her donations to cover these expenses.

Then, one afternoon, while Aimee was driving past Echo Park in Los Angeles she had the strangest feeling that this was the place where she was to build her church. There was a vacant lot directly across from the park. What a wonderful place to build a church. The children could play while waiting for church to begin and her congregation could have picnics after the Sunday morning services. And what a gorgeous view!

She called a real estate agent and was told that the property was not for sale. But that didn't matter because God told her it was hers. Within a week, Aimee had a deal. She had just enough money, saved by her frugal mother, to give the owner a percentage of the down payment. Within four months she closed the deal. Aimee hired a contractor, Brook Hawkins, to begin work on the project. She informed him she would have to build the structure piece by piece as the funding came in. He told her he understood. Although she envisioned a wooden tabernacle, her contractor suggested concrete and stone because of its durability and stability. He also persuaded her to upgrade from her original proposal of 2500 seats to 5000, given the size of the crowds at her crusades. She agreed.

Aimee decided to call her church the Echo Park Revival Tabernacle and she began to solicit donations in *The Bridal Call*. Her mother suggested placing the publication on the newsstands so it would reach a greater audience. Aimee agreed. They had to let people know she needed a significant amount of money, possibly as much as a million dollars. Minnie thought that the best way to increase the amount of money coming in was to increase the size of the crowds. Although Aimee was still terrified of what could happen if the crowds got out of hand, she reluctantly gave in.

Minnie told her they had outgrown the tents and auditoriums and that they should try an outdoor service where the size of the crowd would not be restricted by walls. Minnie received permission from the city park commissioner of San Diego to use Balboa Park, which held the world's only outdoor pipe organ. The city even offered police support, the U.S. marines, and army personnel to direct traffic. In her first two days of services — in January 1921 — 30,000 people filled the park. Her crowds rivalled the size of crowds that U.S. presidents commanded.

Freewill offerings were taken up at all of her revival meetings with the proceeds going toward her building fund. From the San Diego appearance, Aimee collected $5000, enough to dig the hole for the foundation. Aimee immediately sent the funds to Brook Hawkins. Minnie began selling pictures of Aimee for $1 each, miniature chairs for $25, and bags of cement for $5. Fundraising became the primary initiative for the two enterprising women.

Aimee then moved on to St. Louis, where she preached three times a day to crowds of thousands in the Coliseum. Thousands of dollars were coming down the aisles in the freewill offerings and it was all that Minnie could do to keep an eye on the ushers. It often took her until the middle of each night, locked in one of the offices, to finish counting the collection. Then she would rise at 5 a.m. and go right back to the Coliseum to begin organizing the services for the next day. Aimee and Minnie returned to Los Angeles with more than $16,000, enough to pay for the construction of the church's foundation.

Later, in Denver, an interdenominational crowd donated $13,000 toward the construction of her church, and a further $5000 for chairs. While Aimee was in Denver, she had prayed over the Mayor's wife, who had a broken foot. When her foot was completely healed, the woman and her friends gave Aimee their full support. The young evangelist eventually left Denver with over $70,000. The walls of her church were sure to go up.

About this time, Aimee received word that Harold McPherson had been granted a divorce from her. Her conservative followers did not believe in divorce and she was

Thousands seek healing at Aimee Semple McPherson's baptismal services, Oakland, California, August 5, 1922.

nervous about this development. They tried to keep the news from spreading. Aimee refused to comment on the situation or to even think about it. She single-mindedly focused on the building of her new church.

During this same period Aimee discovered a new and unique means of getting her message across. Radio. Back then it was called a "wireless telephone" or just "wireless." Aimee became the first woman to preach a sermon on the wireless. This was fortuitous as the medium was in its infancy and she believed that the possibilities of spreading the gospel, and for her ministry becoming very well known, were measureless. Aimee vowed to do as much radio preaching as possible.

Aimee's ministry began to receive backing from an unusual source. For some time, Aimee had known that members of the Ku Klux Klan were attending her meetings. At this juncture, Aimee thought of them as merely a radical arm of the evangelical movement. She wasn't aware at the time that they were vigilantes so consumed with racial hatred that they actively and secretively committed acts of terror and violence.

At the end of one of her services in Denver, Colorado, in June 1922, a man approached Aimee and informed her that someone in a car needed prayer. Not wanting to go with the man by herself, she asked a female reporter, who happened to be standing in the doorway, to accompany her. As Aimee stuck her head inside the man's car, she and Frances Wayne of the *Denver Post*, were pushed inside. The door was slammed shut behind them and the car took off. They found themselves in the presence of two men in white hoods and robes that Aimee recognized as Klansmen.

One of the men placed blindfolds on the startled women. They wove through many streets for what seemed like an eternity before coming to a stop. Soon they were being led into a hall. After the blindfolds were removed, Aimee saw that the room was filled with hundreds of Klansmen. The men gave Aimee white roses, and praised her for her purity. They assured her of their full support. After this strange and unsettling ceremony the two women were returned unharmed.

During her time in Denver, the king of the Serbian gypsies, Chief Mark, came to Aimee for healing. He had a respiratory disease and his mother had a fibroid tumour. They were both miraculously healed. Chief Mark vowed to devote the next year of his life to Aimee's fundraising drive. He sent letters and telegrams to gypsies all across North America urging them to support her. Hundreds came in caravans to her revivals, showering her with flowers and presents, and calling her the "holy lady." They gave Aimee the gold chains from around their necks, and the gold coins from their pockets. They donated jewels and stained glass and artistry. Their campfires became a familiar sight near Aimee's revival tents. Minnie took the gold and the jewellery, and put it into the building fund.

Shortly before she left Denver, the Ku Klux Klansmen approached her again. This time two Klansman came to her hotel and handed her a bag of money, which they said was for her children.

A month later, Klansmen took Aimee, one of her associates, and a different reporter, from a revival meeting in Oakland to a Klan rally. They then asked her to preach, after which they presented her with a cheque for $100. On another occasion, at her last service in her tent in Oakland, a letter of support from the Ku Klux Klan was read aloud to the congregation. The letter was accompanied by a donation of a further $100 towards the building fund. It wasn't until years later that she learned of the Klan's violent activities and confronted them about their racial prejudice. When she finally did confront them years later — it was from her pulpit — in her home church.

As Aimee was wondering how she should structure her new church, and what kind of doctrinal emphasis it should have, she had a vision. While she was preaching in Oakland in 1922, from the book of Ezekiel, she saw in the four faces described in the Biblical passage — the face of a man, the face of a lion, the face of an ox, and the face of an eagle — clearly, it was a vision of the four faces (or functions) of Jesus Christ. She decided that this representation of Christ was what she wanted her followers to uphold. In the face of a man Aimee saw the Son of man, the One who gave up His life to restore people's relationship with God. In the face of the lion she saw the Lion of the tribe of Judah, as Christ is referred to in the book of Revelations, the One who brings the presence of the Holy Spirit for courage and strength. In the face of the ox she saw Christ as the bearer of burdens and sicknesses, the Healer who brings wholeness to spirit, mind, and body. In the face of the eagle, which swoops down suddenly without warning, she saw Christ as the "coming" King. Aimee fervently believed in the second coming of Christ, the idea that Jesus would someday return physically to the earth to establish a thousand-year reign. Much of what she talked about concerned this coming time of peace and restoration.

Aimee called her doctrinal vision the Foursquare Gospel, and in 1927 she incorporated her branch churches under the name of the International Foursquare Gospel Church. She formed an association of churches called the Foursquare Evangelistic Association. The new church was made up of ministers from a variety of denominational backgrounds that signed a doctrinal statement echoing Aimee's view of the fourfold ministry of Christ. Baptist, Presbyterian, and Congregational ministers, along with a variety of ministers from other churches, affirmed her vision of Christ's roles.

In August 1922, Aimee finally took time off for a long overdue vacation. She set sail for Australia, knowing that the major part of the construction for her church was underway. Now she could rest easy. Her flock would have a stable place to learn her unique brand of evangelism. As she sat on the deck of the ship, enjoying the first real stretch of rest since she had driven across the country four long years before, Aimee began to have visions and dreams about her church. She felt that God was speaking to her, giving her guidance about the nature of her tabernacle.

For the first time, she began to question the name she had chosen. Revival Tabernacle would not aptly describe the vision that God was giving her. He was telling her to build much more than a worship centre. As she prayed on the deck chair in the glorious sun, breathing in the fresh sea air, Aimee envisioned a school for evangelists, a broadcasting centre, a prayer tower, a charitable support system, and the hub of an evangelistic network that would spread out all over the globe. She was sure that God was giving her these visions and dreams — and if He was giving them — she knew that they would come to pass.

She heard bells softly tinkling in the distance. The bells that call people to church ... Catholics called them "angelus bells." Angelus Temple. Of course! Los Angeles! She had her name — Angelus Temple — the church of the bells calling people into the presence of God. Angelus Temple ... the more Aimee said it, the more she liked the sound of the words and the image of the bells. Angelus, angels watching over her, as she believed they always did.

As the ship disembarked Aimee was completely at peace. She already felt well rested, ready to take charge, to lead the charge in the battle for God. Aimee imagined ringing those bells far and wide, the Angelus bells, and the bells of the angels of God.

Chapter 7
The Rise of
the Temple

On New Year's Day, 1923, Aimee got up at dawn to place roses on a float that depicted her precious Angelus Temple. Inside the border of flowers, on the largest truck she could find, were an organ and a small group of singers, ready to belt out rousing hymns. The singers held armfuls of invitations, which they would toss to the spectators at the Tournament of Roses Parade, inviting them to the opening of Angelus Temple at 2:30 that afternoon.

Hours before the opening ceremony, thousands of Aimee's supporters lined the streets outside the round structure, lining up to get inside. There were grandparents, parents, and children, the sick and the healthy, the poor and the rich, and people of all races and colours from all denominations and nationalities. The well dressed and the threadbare stood ready to sing together in joyous celebration.

Give me that old time religion
Give me that old time religion
Give me that old time religion
It's good enough for me!

Police diverted traffic away from the crowd that was beginning to block the streets. Excitement filled the air. The clapping and singing were infectious. There was an intimate party atmosphere, which Aimee always managed to inspire.

Inside the Angelus Temple, a golden harp was being lowered onto the preaching platform. A woman from Australia, a harpist who had come especially for the service, guided it down. As the orchestra tuned up, the volunteer ushers took their places, under Minnie's firm direction, of course.

When the doors opened, the crowd burst in and raced to get one of the 5300 seats. With standing room added, the temple was able to accommodate up to 7500, but the crowd far exceeded that number. Thousands stood outside, straining their ears to hear the glorious music lead by Aimee Semple McPherson and her white-robed choir.

All hail the power of Jesus name
Let angels prostrate fall
Bring forth the royal diadem

And crown Him Lord of all
Bring forth the royal diadem
And crown Him Lord of all.

Minnie was controlling the crowds, making sure that everything was in order — patrolling the doors, the aisles, the stair-
ways — keeping everything running smoothly. Satisfied that
nothing was amiss, she took her seat on the platform next to
Aimee and smiled.

The building had been built. The songs had all been
sung. But that night an exhausted Aimee entered the parsonage and threw herself onto her bed. The hard work had
only just begun. The temple was debt free, but the ongoing
costs were going to be astronomical. There were more than
a dozen employees on the weekly payroll: bookkeepers,
caretakers, office staff, security, etc. And many more would
be hired to run the prayer tower and the evangelistic school
that were in the planning stage. Aimee also wanted a radio
station and a charitable commissary. Her dreams were big,
but so was her budget.

Minnie also felt the pressure. The capable administrator
was used to running a farm, not a corporation. She had left
school at 15, and she had never taken any business courses.
Yet, all of the responsibility for running the temple was
placed squarely upon her shoulders, hiring, training, super-
vising, and firing. She was overwhelmed but dared not hand
any of her authority over to anyone else. Minnie didn't know

whom she could trust: certainly not her daughter, who had never been able to handle practical matters.

Aimee tossed and turned, unable to sleep. She was happy about the parade and the Angelus Temple opening. But she was under more pressure than she had ever faced before. If the crowds didn't come and she missed making the payroll, she would have to go back on the road. And she was far too tired to do that. She decided to preach 23 sermons a week and she knew that she had to make those sermons entertaining. With Hollywood only a few blocks away, at a time when the silent film industry was coming into fruition, Aimee had to come up with stunts that were more appealing than the latest silent film. Her recognition of this resulted in her becoming a very skilled improvisational comedienne. So much so that Charlie Chaplin, Tallulah Bankhead, Agnes DeMille, and other famous stars of the day began to come to her services to study her technique.

Her most popular and well-attended service of the week was on Sunday evenings. It sold out every week because that was the time for the "illustrated sermons," her mini-dramas that became more and more elaborate as time went on. Hundreds had to be turned away each week. The city had to increase the number of streetcars through the Echo Park region immediately before and after Aimee's Sunday night meetings. The idea for the illustrated sermons had come to Aimee in the tent meetings in Florida. But what she did in the tents was far more simplistic than what she was able to do at the temple. In her own church, she hired a set designer with a background in the theatre to work specifically on the sets for her dramas. Aimee also hired people to assist her with the costumes and the lighting. In addition, she befriended theatre artists and talked with them about different ways to approach her work. To top it all off, she wrote musicals and dramas that rivalled those in the theatres.

Actually, this all came quite naturally for Aimee because, before she met Robert Semple in Ingersoll, her ambition had been to become an actress. Perhaps, in achieving her own personal dream, it was easy, albeit challenging, for her to transform her church platform into an elaborate stage. Not since the ancient Greeks had the gods been called forth in such ritual and pageantry. Aimee ordered the best of everything. Large professional orchestras filled the orchestra pit. The actors often wore rich silk fabrics. There was intricate lighting and a state-of-the-art sound system. Broadway producers began to approach Aimee to convince her to appear in their theatres. She turned them down because there was too much work to do at home. Besides, there was absolutely no need to travel to New York when she was experiencing so much success with her own burgeoning production company. Strangely, Aimee was never willing to admit that she was an actress or a producer or that she worked in theatre. She merely stated that she was presenting the gospel message in a medium that was easily accessible to her viewers.

Many of her flock couldn't speak English. Some of her

congregants were Mexicans, who lived in a Spanish-speaking section of Los Angeles. Although they didn't understand the English tongue, they did appreciate the music, the movement, and the costumes, as well as the art form and its pageantry. Part of Aimee's mystique was the ability to recognize that she could move peoples' spirits through a medium they understood and responded to, the arts. People from all walks of life, who couldn't afford to pay for the tickets at secular theatres, came to hers. She didn't charge admission. It was the best deal in town.

The crowd really came alive when Aimee acted out the scriptures. When she developed new productions she always did a test run with her mother as the audience. When they were at home in the house Aimee would dress up in costumes and practice her roles. Although Minnie, who shared the parsonage with her, thought the whole spectacle was ridiculous, she had to admit that the dramas brought in the most enthusiastic crowds of the week.

Roberta loved to watch her mother putting on costumes and playing dress-up. Sometimes they would dress up together and her mother would let her take part in the dramas. Roberta had a very good memory and could be counted on to remember complicated lines. Aimee had helped Roberta to memorize difficult scripture passages since she was about five years old.

Any time the child was confronted by a church member or a board member about her irresponsible, fun-loving prants, Roberta would spout off a scripture verse, transforming herself into the perfect preacher's kid. She used scripture passages to keep sober Christians on their toes and cause them to forget her indiscretions. Roberta had lots of fun imitating her mother, and imagining what it must be like to be a full-grown preacher.

Like her mother, Roberta loved to be the centre of attention, and she quickly became the pastor of the children's church. At the age of 12, she could preach a hefty sermon and hold the children's attention. She also shared her mother's quirky sense of humour and she was known to poke fun at almost anything. Every week, Roberta gave a short command performance to the younger ones, leading them in the song service and keeping them laughing. She was beautiful, bubbly, and enthusiastic. She meant every word she said and she inspired faith and hope in the less fortunate. She was a child with a heart.

The Ku Klux Klan occasionally showed up in their robes at some of her services. They had put a lot of money into the building of the temple. Her falling out with them came about a year after the Temple was built. One night, when hundreds of them began to fill the front rows, Aimee Semple McPherson dared to preach a sermon against racial prejudice.

Roberta was sitting in the pews waiting for the evening service to begin, when her mother rushed in and ordered her to take her brother back to the parsonage. Roberta sensed that something was wrong because the usual attendees were giving up their seats in terror as a large group of white-robed men entered the temple. Although Roberta obeyed her mother and took Rolf home, she quickly returned and hid in the upper balcony.

Roberta knew that the men were members of the Ku Klux Klan, and she wanted to see what her mother was going to do. Although her mother had supported the Klan in earlier years because of their support for traditional values, she knew that Aimee did not approve of their (by now well publicized) treatment of people of other races. Was her mother about to cause a showdown? Roberta felt Aimee just might, and she didn't want to miss a second of it. She sat on the edge of her seat and peered over the balcony to the platform below, straining to see and hear, and praying that her mother couldn't see her. The men in white robes sat erect and stiff with their tall cone-like heads protruding up like pointed spears. Suddenly, Aimee moved forward toward them like a charging stallion. She launched into a well known story about a coloured farmer who longed to enter a beautiful "white" church. Her voice was loud and full, and her words were pronounced with great conviction ...

... the farmer tried to enter the church, and an usher threw him out. As he sat on the steps in despair, a stranger approached him and commiserated with him. The stranger told him that he too had been thrown out of that church. It was only in later reflection, that the farmer realized the stranger had been Christ.

Aimee confronted the Klan on their racial prejudice that night — and one by one they left — leaving their robes behind them on the floor. After they were gone, and before her mother noticed her presence, Roberta slipped away too and went home. She had never been so proud of her mother. It took an immense courage to confront such a large number of burly men. Roberta sensed a new and powerful strength of purpose in her mother. Aimee was clearly ready to confront the evils around her. At that moment, Roberta wasn't sure that she was ready to follow her mother into battle.

Meanwhile Rolf, who had never been afraid of anything, was waiting to hear all about it. As he sat listening to Roberta unfold the tale of what his mother had done, he wasn't at all surprised. He knew the strength of his mother and he knew even then that he too, when the time was right, would stand up against any individual or group — no matter how powerful.

Rolf had never had a desire to fit in or to please people the way Roberta had. He was aware that he was on the fringes of society because his mother was an evangelical preacher, but he didn't mind. He had never wanted to become mainstream. He was simply thankful that people treated him well and that he had a warm place to sleep. Simple pleasures satisfied Rolf. He didn't have to face the deeper questions that his sister did. He didn't have to understand why or how. He just accepted things the way they were. He was happy.

When their mother returned home, the whole family, including Minnie, talked about the Klan in relation to Christian values. Then they discussed consequences that might arise due to Aimee's challenge that night. Aimee knew that church revenues would go down because of the stance she had taken, but she didn't care. As always, she trusted God to provide for her. And she knew she had done the right thing. Minnie wasn't so sure. Sometimes she thought that Aimee should just keep her mouth shut and let other folks fight the battles for her. She knew that racial prejudice wasn't right but she didn't think it would do any good to poke a serpent with a stick.

Rolf hugged his mother and told her how proud of her he was and that he would stand up for her no matter what happened. Aimee kissed his forehead and held him tight. She was so glad she had had this second child. Although she no longer wanted anything to do with his father, and was beginning to realize that the marriage was a mistake from the beginning, she loved Rolf with all her heart. Her little boy was solid and true and she knew he always would be.

Roberta, on the other hand, was becoming more and more like her grandmother every day. Aimee often wished she had never had to leave the child with Minnie when she had first gone out on the road. Minnie had distorted her. Roberta was often more interested in pleasing people than in pleasing God — just like Minnie. Aimee knew it was too late now. The damage had been done.

Aimee had a sermon to prepare. She had little time to

worry about Minnie and her foibles. So, once more, she left the children in Minnie's care and got back to work. She knew she had to come up with a more elaborate plan, one that would make it possible to replace the lost revenue that the departure of the Klan and their supporters would undoubtedly result in. Aimee forgot about her sermon for a while and spent some time thinking about ways to do this.

Later than night, Aimee had an idea. What about using animals in the dramas? They always brought in a crowd. She could rent a few camels and sheep. That's it! She would play the shepherdess in the parable of the lost sheep. Where could she get a sheep? Somebody must know. There had to be sheep in the countryside somewhere. And she could use a camel for the parable of the rich man, whom Christ compared to a camel unable to crawl through the eye of a needle with burdens on his back. She could construct a tunnel and have a live camel crawl through it! What about a talking bird? A macaw? Perhaps she could rent one from a circus for a sequence about the Garden of Eden.

The next week Aimee rented a macaw. She was so excited about having the beautiful bird gracing her stage, that is, until it told her to go to hell. For a moment she thought she had heard wrong, so she decided she must have been mistaken and hoped for the best. The Sunday night illustrated sermon went on as scheduled. The macaw looked majestic and it was keeping its mouth shut.

But when Aimee was in the middle of her sermon, the

bird called out in a loud clear voice, "Go to hell!" Instead of the quiet regal bird she thought she had acquired, Aimee had a centre stage heckler. The crowd roared. Determined not to let this bird get the better of her, she decided on the spot to include the bird's antics as part of the act, and used the bird as an example of bad behaviour. The congregation had no idea that the stunt had not been planned. Aimee was a genius at improvisation.

One month after the temple opened, Aimee held her first training course for budding evangelists. The class of 50 students met from Tuesday morning through Friday morning in the overflow prayer room. As the months wore on, more and more students joined them. Aimee was the primary teacher. Later, when the courses expanded to several hundred students, she hired an interdenominational faculty to teach such subjects as homiletics, social service work, pastoral visitation, and doctrinal issues. Her intention was to launch a series of Foursquare Gospel Churches, first in North America and then all over the world. She planned to train ministers in her school to pastor these churches so that these missionaries would become the "salt of the earth," and heat up the religious fervour in the areas they served.

Male and female candidates were equally considered for ordination, as were people from a wide variety of denominational backgrounds, educational levels, ages, and races. Aimee always made room for promising candidates. All she asked is that potential students have a heart open to God, an experience of revivalism, and a willingness to serve. From the beginning she stressed the Salvation Army method of serving the poor. Aimee wanted practical workers, not talkers. She told her students they had to act out the gospel, not just talk about it. They had to make themselves useful and serve, not only the people who might join their churches, but anyone in need.

Aimee never insisted that those who received her help or her healing prayers should believe in the same way that she believed. She served people because they were human beings. Aimee believed that all human beings were made in the image of God and that each person deserved to be treated as if though he or she were Christ himself. Right from the time they signed up for the course, she sent her students out into the streets to serve those in need. Students from her Lighthouse of International Foursquare Evangelism (LIFE) Bible College (as she later called it) held noon hour services in prisons, in hospitals, and even workplaces. Her students were very active in the greater community, not just in holding spiritual meetings, but also in performing charitable works.

A year after the temple opened, Aimee oversaw construction of the six-storey LIFE Bible College, next to the temple administration building. Meanwhile, during the second month of the temple's operation, the 24-hours-a-day, seven-days-a-week, prayer tower opened. Volunteers took prayer requests by telephone, by mail, and by telegraph. The prayer shifts were two hours long, with the women working the day shift and the men working the night shift.

Right from the time the temple opened, Aimee had held special services for children. Her daughter's talented speaking brought a good crowd to the children's church. Roberta had her father's fine qualities; she was a strikingly beautiful 12-year-old, well spoken, intelligent, and sensitive. Her passions were music, reading, and public speaking. Aimee thought she would make a natural pastor and she began to groom her daughter to take over the pulpit after she was gone.

Rolf had never expressed any desire to become a pastor. Even though he was the man of the family, the 10-year-old boy preferred to be in the background, quietly tinkering with machinery or studying mathematics. His desire was to be an electrical engineer. Aimee hoped that he would someday take over the business side of the operation and perform the administrative duties. But even at this young age Rolf clearly preferred the technical and secular side of things to anything mystical or mysterious. He had no problem with his mother's plan of making Roberta her successor in the pulpit.

Aimee was quite confident that her future was secure with her two talented children there to take over when she and Minnie retired. She placed a heavy responsibility on both of them to attend services and to carry their weight when it came to the work around the temple. The two of them became dependable helpers as well as role models for the temple's young people.

In 1924, still excited by the experience she had had on the radio in 1922, Aimee decided to build her own broadcasting centre. "Wireless" was still a very new concept when Aimee lobbied to obtain her broadcasting licence. The greatest obstacle was that she was a woman. No woman had ever owned her own radio station in the United States, and the authorities were not entirely sure that one should. As usual, Aimee won out in the end and was granted the first licence ever given to a woman. When her station KFSG opened on February 6, 1924, it became the first religious broadcasting station in the United States. The station's opening audience was estimated to be in excess of 200,000 people.

Subsequently, Aimee's followers came through with the $25,000 needed to install the radio station on the third floor of the temple building. A radio engineer, Kenneth Ormiston, was hired to construct and run the facility at the grand salary of $3000 a year. As soon as KSFG was up and running, Aimee went on "live" every morning at 7 a.m. with a show called *The Sunshine Hour*. Her daily programming included live broadcasts of her sermons, inspirational messages, music concerts, a teaching series, readings, and news commentaries. Aimee encouraged her converts to go on the radio and "testify" about what God had done for them, and she made her station an indelible part of community life in Los Angeles. It was a station of the people and for the people. The station was down to earth, upbeat, grassroots, and creative.

However, it wasn't long until problems began to gather on the horizon. Aimee spent so much time at the station — getting it launched, overseeing it, and going on live — she forgot that she had another life. Radio became her obsession. It was her baby and it needed constant care. However, in Minnie's opinion, she became a little too friendly with the radio operator. No wonder, Kenneth was the first person Aimee saw every morning and the last person she saw at night. She relied on his expertise to guide her every move, and she gobbled up information like a hungry child. Aimee was sure that radio was going to open up her ministry to the modern world. Knowledge of the medium would be the key to her continued success.

Minnie didn't understand Aimee's obsession at all. To her, radio was just another worldly preoccupation, like the theatre. Besides, it might take Aimee's eyes and thoughts off God. Minnie tried valiantly to pull Aimee away from Kenneth and the broadcasting arena and for more than one reason. A complication, which could have serious repercussions, was that Kenneth was married and had children. In addition, he was rumoured to have had numerous affairs. The radio technician had never professed to support evangelical Christianity. In fact, he seemed to mock it. But Aimee enjoyed Kenneth's company, and he made her laugh. She found most of the people around the temple far too serious, and they didn't fully appreciate her artistic flair. Kenneth, on the other hand, was creative and intelligent. He loved her theatrical antics, and he appreciated a side of her that her mother never had.

The two shared a dry sense of humour and a keen perception of society, which many of Aimee's flock might never have understood ... or liked. Kenneth may have seen a side of Aimee that she seldom showed to anyone else. They began to communicate over the telephone intercom during Aimee's services, with Kenneth in the broadcasting centre on the third floor and Aimee on the preaching platform. Kenneth would make snide remarks about the antics of people getting carried away with emotionalism in their worship. Aimee would respond to his comments. Although the two thought that these "sound checks" were private communications, people on the second balcony often overheard them, and they began to complain to Minnie. Aimee's flock did not like the familiar tone that was evolving between this married man and their preacher.

Minnie finally exploded, ordering Aimee to stay away from Kenneth. She banned her daughter from associating with the cynical secularist. He was destroying her credibility with her congregation. Well, that just added fuel to Aimee's fire. She was not going to allow her mother to order her around. She told Minnie that it was her life and she would live it her own way. After all, she was almost 35 years old. Nevertheless, by the end of the year, ostensibly under pressure from Minnie, Kenneth Ormiston resigned. Aimee went on an extended visit to the Holy Land with Roberta.

By the time she returned several months later, Minnie had absolute reign over the temple. Aimee faced a torrent of complaints about Minnie's method of management from a number of the temple employees. Some of the complaints were anonymous and some were not. But Minnie found out who they were and each and every one of them was quickly dismissed. Aimee chose to look the other way.

Shortly after arriving back at the temple, Aimee held a slide show of her trip to the Holy Land. Coloured slides were a new innovation and, as a result, hundreds of people were fighting to get in. So Aimee, ever the crowd pleaser, promised she would return the next night and show them again. The second slide show never took place.

The next day, May 18, 1926, Aimee and her secretary, Emma Shaffer, went to Ocean Park Beach. Late in the afternoon Aimee headed into the waves. She was a strong swimmer and often went swimming to relax. This was nothing unusual and Emma didn't think anything of it. However, she began to get concerned when she could no longer see Aimee out in the ocean. She moved closer down to the shore but still didn't see any sign of her employer. Now she was really worried and asked others on the beach to watch for Aimee while she went to a neighbouring hotel and called the police. Then she called the temple office. By the time the police arrived, Emma was completely distraught and was convinced that Aimee had drowned. Minnie tearfully told the crowds that had gathered at the temple that night to see Aimee's slide show that her daughter was "with Jesus."

Chapter 8
A Time of Turmoil

he Los Angeles police conducted a full-scale search with airplanes, glass-bottomed boats, police dogs, deep-sea divers, and dragging equipment. A vigil of thousands of Aimee's followers remained at Ocean Park Beach for days, singing and praying.

The police received tips about supposed sightings of Aimee from all over North America. There were also a few letters from people saying they had kidnapped Aimee and demanding ransom. None of these turned out to be credible. They had no strong leads until Mrs. Ormiston, Kenneth's wife, filed a missing person report regarding her husband. The police knew that Ormiston had been romantically linked with the evangelist. Could the two disappearances be connected?

Working Miracles

Later, when Kenneth Ormiston himself turned up to dispel the rumours, the police dropped that line of investigation. The radio operator said he had not seen Aimee since he had left his employment at the temple almost six months earlier.

About a month after Aimee disappeared, Minnie decided to hold a memorial service. Minnie preached Aimee's eulogy on June 20 to an overflow crowd. She hoped that her daughter would finally be laid to rest, even though the coroner's office refused to issue a death certificate because there was no body. Minnie's peace was short-lived. Three days after the memorial service, the police arrived at Minnie's door to tell her that her daughter had been found alive.

While the police were still there, Minnie received a call from Aimee herself. She told her mother she had been kidnapped and held for ransom. Deputy District Attorney, Joseph Ryan and Chief of Detectives, Herman Cline, as well as Minnie and Aimee's two children, headed out to Douglas, Arizona, to find out the truth of the matter.

Aimee poured out her story from her hospital bed. The evangelist said that after swimming for about an hour at Ocean Beach, she walked up onto the sand and dried herself off. A young couple approached her and asked her to come and pray for their dying baby, who was in their car. When she got to the car, Aimee saw a woman in the back seat holding in her arms what appeared to be a baby. When she attempted to approach the child, Aimee was pushed from behind, and a rag with some sort of anaesthetic was held over her nose and mouth. Aimee claimed she lost consciousness as the car sped away.

When she awoke, her hands and feet were tied, and she was in a cabin with a woman and two men. They told her they were holding her for ransom. A few weeks later, when they left her alone for the first time, she managed to free her hands by rolling from the bed and cutting the ropes on a rusty can. She then escaped by walking for several hours through the desert until she came to an isolated cabin filled with Mexicans. They took her to the authorities in the small Mexican town of Agua Prieta where she convinced the authorities to take her across the state line into Arizona. From there she called for help.

The police questioned Aimee over and over, and Minnie could understand why. The story just didn't add up. They asked her why her shoes were not worn down from trudging through the sand, and why there were no sand grains on the insides. Why were her clothes not filled with perspiration from walking through the desert? Why was her skin not sun-burned? And why didn't she show any signs of dehydration?

Minnie couldn't make up her mind what to believe. She knew her daughter was impetuous but she had never thought that she was a liar. Had she run off with that married man? Minnie had never trusted Ormiston. Aimee and Ormiston had disappeared at the same time. Minnie paced up and down in front of Aimee's hospital bed thinking this way and that, running through all the possibilities in her mind. Finally, she came to a conclusion. In order to save the ministry and the temple, no matter what she suspected, she would have to back Aimee one hundred percent. If Aimee said there was a kidnapping — there was a kidnapping — evidence or not.

The police were running out of patience and clearly did not believe Aimee. They were looking for something, any tangible evidence to pin Aimee's story on. They couldn't locate the Mexicans whom Aimee said had helped her cross the border, nor could they find the cabin she was imprisoned in. They couldn't find any tracks through the sand that could have been hers, other than a trail that led only a few kilometres from the edge of the desert and disappeared into some car tracks. They looked as though someone had climbed out of a car and walked into town. There was not a shred of evidence that the faith healer had been through an ordeal in the desert.

When they returned to Los Angeles, Aimee and Minnie were charged with corrupting the public morals and they were asked to testify before the grand jury. It was District Attorney Asa Keye's conviction that Aimee had used her disappearance as a publicity stunt to raise her profile and make money, and that her mother had gone right along with it. Minnie told the district attorney that his notions were ridiculous. There was no insurance policy on Aimee's life and no mortgage on the temple. The organization was not in need of money. There was no need for shenanigans, she stated.

During the initial search off Ocean Park Beach, a deep-sea diver had died of exposure trying to locate Aimee in the

Pacific Ocean. If the two women had knowingly misled the public, Keyes was prepared to throw the book at them. For months he tried to convict them of foul play, but eventually he had to drop the charges due to insufficient evidence.

But the press was not satisfied. Investigative journalists were looking for hard evidence about what had really happened to Aimee Semple McPherson. While the legal system gave up its relentless pursuit, the press never did. Many journalists felt that this miracle worker, to whom they had given their trust, was lying to them. They wanted the truth and they would stop at nothing to find it. Most of them refused to accept that Aimee had, in fact, been kidnapped. They wouldn't have minded if she had had an affair and confessed it. They didn't expect her to be as perfect as her congregation might have. They were secularists who accepted the foibles of humanity. What they couldn't abide was that her evidence didn't add up. There was nothing to back up her story of being kidnapped. They were sure she had been somewhere else, possibly with Kenneth Ormiston. Throughout the 1920s, the stories about the evangelist in the press had almost all been positive, but now the articles that filled the newspapers and magazines were examining her in a different light. They viewed her as someone desperate, confused, and even unscrupulous. It wasn't long before they found something tangible to write about.

A few days after the charges were dropped against Aimee and Minnie, several witnesses came forward claiming that they had seen Aimee with Ormiston at a cottage in Carmel, California. They produced a grocery list in Aimee's handwriting, as well as books that contained passages that Aimee had quoted in her sermons. There was also a trunk full of fine clothing that had been purchased at stores Aimee was known to frequent. A mysterious Mrs. McInyre had left them behind.

The press went wild writing stories about the supposed affair until a woman called Loraine Wiseman stepped forward and swore it was her sister, not Aimee, that had been with Ormiston. That took the heat off Aimee, until a short time later, when Loraine Wiseman was arrested for writing bad cheques. When Minnie refused to pay her bail, Loraine claimed that Minnie and Aimee had hired her to lie to the investigators about her sister. At that point the district attorney charged Aimee Semple McPherson, Minnie Kennedy, and Loraine Wiseman, each with three counts of perjury.

Day after day endless witnesses, who told implausible stories about her alleged rendezvous with Ormiston in Carmel, dragged Aimee's name through the mud. Then Loraine changed her story, saying that Aimee and Minnie had never bribed her. The charges against the two were dropped. There were accusations made that both Loraine and Asa Keyes had been paid off. Keyes was later convicted of taking a bribe in an unrelated case and was sent to San Quentin (where Aimee later visited him).

Meanwhile the temple staff put out the word that Aimee

had been a victim of the mob. Mob figures had been threatening her ever since the temple opened because she had converted drug dealers and prostitutes who, subsequently, turned in their bosses. Minnie thought that the mob would have been more likely to kill Aimee to silence her, than to have kidnapped her. But Aimee's attorney had been found mysteriously dead in an overturned car, and one of her researchers had, very questionably, committed suicide. So, the temple staff continued to blame organized crime for the kidnapping and Minnie kept her mouth shut. She really couldn't decide whether or not her daughter had, deliberately, initiated the mob story. Aimee never discounted the rumours.

The day after the charges against her were dropped, Aimee decided to go on a cross-country tour that the press dubbed her "vindication tour." Minnie begged her not to go, saying that the temple needed her presence after the long courtroom ordeal. But Aimee insisted, taking several "protectors" with her to hold off the press and keep the crowds away. Minnie decided to remain at the temple in an effort to keep the ship on a straight course.

Aimee appears fearful, nervous, and agitated in the pictures taken of her around this time. Her cheeks are hollowed out and her eyes appear haunted and desperate. In an attempt to improve her appearance she bobbed her hair in the latest style and adopted the fashions of the 1920s.

While in New York, she visited nightclubs and dance halls, claiming she was finding new prospects for her church.

But the things that used to bother her no longer seemed to prick her conscience. She watched others drink, smoke, and dance at The Three Hundred Club until long after midnight without an eye of condemnation, and she adopted the language of someone acquainted with the harsher side of life.

Aimee Semple McPherson was no longer the person she had been and she was not sure who she was becoming. She no longer fit in; not with her fundamentalist flock, who thought she might be "tainted" from the kidnapping; not with these drinking and dancing secularists, who didn't understand her God; and not with her family, who felt shut out and abandoned by her emotional withdrawal from them.

Aimee left the nightclub in confusion and wandered the streets hoping to get tired enough to be able to sleep. If only she could rest. Nothing seemed to help, not sleeping pills, not shots of medication, not even prayers. She seemed to be waiting for something, perhaps for Robert Semple to appear and take her out of this trouble, or waiting for Jesus to come in the rapture and take her to Heaven. Aimee Semple McPherson was waiting to be rescued by someone. Anyone.

Lonely and alone, Aimee returned to Los Angeles. Her accompanying party never knew how bad she felt. She never told them. And when Minnie saw her hair and her clothes, and heard the way Aimee was talking, she exploded full force. Aimee was far too tired to argue, far too tired to care about anything anymore. Aimee told Minnie that if she disliked her new image that much, she could resign from, or maybe even leave, Angelus Temple. Aimee didn't want people around her who didn't fully support her.

A few days later, Minnie held a secret meeting of the board of directors, which was composed of seven male elders of the temple. She asked the board to remove Aimee as their pastoral minister, because her daughter had become too "worldly" and sinful. But Aimee walked in on the group unexpectedly. It was obvious what was going on and she demanded they take a vote, either the board approve of her new appearance and her lifestyle or she would resign. She knew she had them over a barrel. There was no one who could replace her. She was the "star" that everyone was coming to see. The temple could always find another business manager but they could not so easily find another star that could fill the seats and pay the bills. The bills were now over $7000 a week. The board, overwhelmingly, voted to keep her.

Minnie resigned in 1927. She demanded half of the temple's assets, but the amount she received was never disclosed. It was estimated to be over $100,000. She told Aimee that if she decided to run the business alone it would become bankrupt in no time. The temple's choirmaster also left. He started his own church, claiming that the temple was worshipping "the god of materialism." Over 300 hundred members left with him, along with most of the musicians.

Aimee suffered under the blow. Her children were not old enough to help her yet and there was no one she could count on. She was so eager for companionship that she trusted everyone who came to her. One after another, shady businessmen convinced Aimee to endorse fantastical schemes such as a cemetery, a hotel, a camp, and a resort. Aimee signed the papers believing that somehow the schemes would work out even if she didn't have the money to support them. Then, when she failed to follow through on her commitments, she was sued again and again.

In 1930, after a three-year absence, Minnie returned to the temple to prevent it from falling into bankruptcy. It was now the Great Depression, and Aimee's followers no longer had money to bail her out. As soon as the temple was moving toward solid ground, Minnie came to the parsonage to give Aimee her resignation. Minnie told her daughter she would not work for a woman whose morals and lifestyle differed so strongly from the gospel of Christ. Aimee cautioned her to lower her voice. There were others in the house. Minnie refused to be shushed and the two women moved their conversation out onto the back patio.

Minnie continued her assault on Aimee's character — accusing her of reading secular books, going to worldly plays and concerts, and befriending theatre artists — things no self-respecting evangelical preacher would do. Aimee told Minnie that the world was changing and that she was changing with it. She had to keep up with the times, in order to reach the people she served. Minnie told her that that was nonsense. And how could she have bobbed her hair? Bobbed hair was a sign of the devil's influence. Minnie seldom mentioned the devil. Aimee felt that blow like a kick to her stomach. And she struck back.

No one saw or heard what occurred next. There are contradictory accounts of what happened. But there are photographs, which were published in the Los Angeles newspapers, of Minnie Kennedy in a hospital bed in the Brentwood Sanatorium, with a wing-shaped bandage over her broken nose. Some accounts say she claimed her daughter hit her. Others accounts say that her nose was bandaged from plastic surgery she had had the day before. It was often said that mother and daughter never saw each other in person again.

Aimee had a nervous collapse. She retreated to a rented cottage in Malibu Beach, where she lost 40 pounds, experienced hysterical blindness, and suffered acute insomnia. She did not return to the pulpit for 10 months.

In the winter of 1931, Aimee left on an around the world cruise with Roberta. The sea had always calmed Aimee's nerves. As they cruised through the Mediterranean Sea in March, she wondered if she could ever go back to that three-ring circus she called a temple. Roberta, too, was looking for escape. At only 20 years of age, she fell in love with the ship's purser, William Smythe, and married him after having known him for only a couple of months. As the two honeymooned, Aimee was left to vacation on her own.

While in Marseilles, Aimee heard that the famous Charlie Chaplin was in town. Longing to speak to someone in English, Aimee arrived at his hotel room door unannounced. Although at first taken aback, Chaplin was soon charmed by the effervescent evangelist and escorted her on a walking tour about the town. Chaplin coyly admitted to Aimee that he had listened to her Sunday night illustrated sermons discreetly from his car, and that he considered her to be one of the finest actresses alive. Although he was a confirmed atheist, he was astounded by the healings he had seen take place in her services, and in the power she commanded over the crowds. He was thoroughly convinced that she was a skilled hypnotist.

Aimee insisted that she was neither an actress nor a hypnotist, but a simple woman used by God. Chaplin countered that preachers are the consummate actors, and that she was one of the greatest he had ever seen. Chaplin accompanied the charming evangelist on a stroll every evening while her ship was docked in Marseilles. He told Aimee, as they strolled along the pier, that he loved her passionate enthusiasm and love of life. He was not at all convinced that Aimee was a fundamentalist. He thought she was an astute performer with an uncanny ability to read crowds.

When Roberta returned to the ship, she found her mother in a better mood than she had been in for years. Roberta even accused her of being in love. Aimee told her she wasn't in love, that she had simply been entertained. But she may never have told her daughter who the famous entertainer had been. Roberta and Aimee returned from their world cruise in time to prepare for another family wedding.

Rolf was engaged to marry his 20-year-old sweetheart, Lorna Dee Smith, whom he had met in Aimee's Evangelical Training School. He was only 18. In June, his mother conducted the two-hour service at the temple.

Even Minnie heard wedding bells in 1931. She married a man from Washington State. Apparently, Aimee was sorry to hear that the marriage was short lived. The man was already married. Although she had not seen her mother since the big fight, and had no intentions of ever seeing her again, Aimee didn't wish her any ill will.

Aimee began to nurture a new relationship of her own, with a man 11 years her junior. David Hutton was playing the role of the Pharaoh in a musical about Moses, which Aimee had composed. Through rehearsing together, Aimee had fallen for the heavy imposing baritone. Although others did not recognize his charms, Aimee thought he was solid and uncompromising. These were also qualities she had admired in Harold McPherson.

While many may have realized that Hutton was not an appropriate match for her, Aimee appears to have been deeply smitten, gazing lovingly into his eyes in photographs and speaking very positively about him to the press. One evening in September, reporters who were visiting the couple dared them to go off and elope. Rolf was stunned when she accepted their dare. The couple flew off to Arizona on a chartered plane. They were married and were back in time for Aimee to preach a sermon the next day.

Divorce and remarriage was still strictly forbidden in evangelical circles at that time. Evangelicals did not remarry if a former spouse were still alive. Harold McPherson was alive, remarried, and living in Florida. Oddly, he counted on Aimee's support cheque every month to keep him financially afloat. Aimee's flock was well aware of this and the board of directors didn't know what to say. But they finally came out in approval of her new marriage. Perhaps the board members felt that they had no other choice. She was still bringing in the crowds at a time of great financial burden.

But many members of her congregation did not approve and they left the fold. Most of them however, did not, believing somehow that anything Aimee did was okay. Miracles were still happening in her services. Wasn't that a sign that she was in God's favour? Many people had come to the temple because of the manifestations of the miraculous. If miraculous healings were still taking place when Aimee prayed, what did it matter who their minister was married to? It was her business. Others in the congregation were just there to be entertained.

Several of her branch churches rebelled. Thirty-two of her ministers in Iowa and Minnesota broke their association with the temple and formed their own churches. Many students who had graduated from her training school began to pull away from her. She also lost many of her followers who had come from mainstream denominations. The old established churches, which were more formal and traditional, believed in sticking to the rules and in social propriety. Their members expected Christian ministers to be above reproach, and they found Aimee's relationship with a much younger man questionable. They also did not like the fact that she had always told her flock that divorce and remarriage was wrong, and now she had done that very thing.

A number of ministers and members of the Methodist, Presbyterian, and Baptist churches did not want to be associated with a moral scandal. Many people from these churches had supported her throughout the kidnapping ordeal, because her story had never been proven wrong. But her marriage to Hutton appeared to be a straightforward refusal to live by moral Christian standards, and it showed a lack of common sense. Divorced people did not remarry while their spouses were still alive, and that was that. She had become a social leper as far as they were concerned, miracles or no miracles.

Just when things were about as bad as they could get, fuel was added to the fire. A few days after Aimee married Hutton, a massage nurse, Myrtle St. Pierre, sued him for breach of promise. She told the press that Hutton had been engaged to her when he began courting Aimee. Hutton told Aimee it wasn't true. By this time, Aimee had already become somewhat disenchanted with her new husband. He was demanding to be put in full control of the temple and Aimee was not so sure that was a good idea. Many of the staff were complaining to her about him, saying that he was rude, overbearing, and disrespectful.

Working Miracles

The stress was just too much for her and Aimee began to get sick. She was in the hospital when she was informed that Myrtle St. Pierre had won her breach of promise suit. Hutton then callously told Aimee that he was lucky to have gotten off with $5000. On hearing this, the startled evangelist fainted and cracked her skull.

As soon as she got out of the hospital, Aimee announced publicly that she had made a mistake marrying Hutton. She apologized to her followers for letting them down and she promised that she would never marry again. In spite of her change of heart, most of those who left never came back. The miracle worker, Aimee Semple McPherson, had failed to regain their trust.

Chapter 9
Repentance — Seclusion — Silence

imee decided that the best way to alleviate her own suffering was to ease the pain of others. In 1933, just after leaving Hutton, Aimee threw herself wholeheartedly into the work of alleviating the distress of the Great Depression. Always having had a generous heart, she now felt even more compelled to help the suffering because she was suffering herself.

Aimee took in elderly men, whose social security benefits had eroded with the stock market crash, allowing them to sleep in her garage. She invited malnourished women, who had come west to avoid the dust storms and drought of Okalahoma, to sleep on her living room floor. When the parents of unwed pregnant teenagers turned them out, she invited the girls into the parsonage and later, as often as not, convinced the parents to take in their daughters and grand-children, after the babies were born.

Although Aimee had launched her Commissary, the social service division of her ministry, back in 1927, she took a keen interest in running it herself after the turmoil of the break up with her mother and her third marriage. Through this period she began to realize that she had inherited some of her mother's organizational skills. Aimee had never been very interested in developing the business side of her personality. As long as her mother was around she didn't have to. But in her social service endeavours, Aimee experienced a heightened sense of well being through the act of bringing joy to others. The simplest things began to give her pleasure; for example, to be able to donate blankets to a baby; to integrate a Mexican citizen into the American way of life; and to be able to feed thousands of people, who had no means of support, each day. Aimee concentrated less on preaching in the 1930s, and more on giving. She realized that in giving she was sending out a strong message of the love of God.

She personally selected the mature godly women who ran the Commissary, and she worked side-by-side with them. Aimee did not turn anyone away that needed help. The county refused to assist anyone who had been a resident of California for less than one year, so the police and fire department brought people, who had nowhere else to turn, to the Commissary. Hundreds of Mexicans, who had come into the country without proper identification, turned to Aimee as their last hope. No government social service agency would help them.

One person who came to offer his help to Aimee was a teenager who later became film star. His name was Anthony Quinn. Although he was reluctant to have anything to do with a Protestant church because he was a devout Catholic, his grandmother convinced the teen to help the lovely lady who had nursed her back to health. Quinn became Aimee's translator in the Mexican community, and he played the saxophone in her band. Before long he began preaching on street corners in his native tongue, developing the outstanding public speaking ability that would soon make him a famous Hollywood star.

Aimee expected all of her flock to help the poor. "Whatsoever you do to the least of these my brethren you do unto me," she reminded them. She said that people must look upon every person as though that person were Christ. Aimee convinced meat packers, bakers, and grocers to donate meat, tinned food, potatoes, and bread. Orchard owners brought fruit and mattress companies sent mattresses. Aimee had an overwhelming influence on those who had more than they needed, and she knew what to say to make them part with it.

Those who were unemployed or retired became her stalwart volunteers. She organized them into a number of different jobs: sorting donations, sewing and mending garments, fixing household items, providing office assistance, and delivering food or other items. Dozens of volunteers sorted through donated canned goods, clothing, furniture, blankets, and bedding. Everything was divided into categories to be prepared for distribution into hampers. Volunteers washed what needed to be cleaned, patched holes where they could, and threw out what could not be restored. A team of seamstresses sewed quilts and made children's clothing and baby layettes with the use of 20 donated sewing machines.

Aimee was known for providing the fastest help in the city. While other social service agencies stalled the process with line-ups and paper trails, Aimee immediately met each need. Within an hour of calling for help, a volunteer from the temple, with no questions asked, would show up at the person's door. A reporter for the *Harold Examiner* said her social service network was among the most accessible and efficient in the city. Scores of volunteers manned the phones around the clock to take down information from those who called for help: asking people's addresses, finding out the number of people in the household, identifying their specific needs, and verifying times for delivery of items.

Aimee organized an army of young volunteers to deliver baskets of food and medicines to the shut-ins. She even convinced the police to deliver goods when she was short of volunteers. She had a team of sympathetic truckers who spent their off-hours taking furniture and larger items to the desperate. Another group of volunteers manned an employment bureau where people were coached to improve their job-search skills. Others helped them to improve their

English skills. Immigrants studied office skills while they learned about the United States.

The temple's soup kitchen was one of the earliest to open, and one of the largest facilities in the city. When the school system could no longer afford to give children a free lunch Aimee stepped in to provide it, on top of her regular feeding of the destitute. In the first month it was open, Aimee's soup kitchen is estimated to have served more than 80,000 meals. Countless volunteers prepared the food, cleaned the facility, and served the needy.

Aimee also established a free medical clinic with a volunteer staff of doctors, dentists, and nurses. To co-operate in the effort, 500 new nurses were trained. And Aimee may have been responsible for convincing the federal government to reopen an abandoned army facility east of the city to provide housing for 25,000 homeless people. Aimee truly fulfilled her legacy by becoming "the angel" of Angelus Temple and of Los Angeles.

Aimee also used her radio station to bring assistance to the troubled and needy. More than once she cancelled her regular programming to ask her listeners to bring provisions in to the temple. And this wasn't a first for her radio station. When a devastating earthquake hit Santa Barbara back in 1925, Aimee had gone live in the early morning requesting canned goods, bedding, and clothing to be brought immediately to the temple. Then she asked for drivers to come and transport the goods, and for others to come and sort and pack the supplies. Aimee's aid reached Santa Barbara before the social service agencies had even been alerted to the fact that there was a problem. Then in 1934, when an earthquake hit Long Beach, Aimee mobilized her helpers more quickly and efficiently than any other agency did. National social service organizations began to approach Aimee about how to facilitate their own relief efforts.

But all of this was very costly and Aimee's flock was not rich. More than one out of every five workers in Los Angeles was on some form of relief. Everyone had relatives, friends, or neighbours who were poor. They simply did not have the money to support Aimee's work. She was having trouble meeting the bills to feed and clothe so many needy people. In short, the temple was beginning to go under. In addition to the ongoing financial pressure, Aimee had had to buy out Minnie's interest in the organization. And she had had to deal with the lawsuits of shady and questionable businessmen. Never the business manager her mother was, Aimee once again found herself in debt. This time it was serious. There was talk of foreclosure by the creditors.

Aimee believed that a radical need demanded a radical solution, and Broadway presented a possible way out. Broadway producers had been begging her to take part in a vaudeville show for years. This time she said yes. She was promised $5000 a week. Aimee was given 10 minutes to speak at the end of a set of vaudeville acts, five times a day. The producers were hoping she would talk about the kidnapping, her divorces, and her fights with her mother.

Instead she talked about the story of her life, her Canadian upbringing, and her evangelistic healing work. She was hoping to convert people, not to entertain them. The producers cancelled her after one week.

Hutton, meanwhile, was launching a vaudeville show of his own — not far away from her on Broadway where he was singing — and telling tales about his life at Angelus Temple. This failed to rattle Aimee. Nothing Hutton said could hurt her. She had left him behind, the way she had left Harold behind so many years before. She was determined to focus on answering the call of God, and on going back to doing what she knew best.

Aimee lost no time in organizing a string of preaching engagements across the United States and set about polishing her "illustrated sermons." She was as popular as ever. Money began to roll back into the temple, and the ministry gained strength once more. But Aimee realized that she could not be away for months at a time without the temple suffering in her absence. Several of the illustrious guest speakers she had brought in over the years had decided to establish rival churches close to hers, and of course, they raided her flock for members.

Aimee decided to hire a woman who had worked with her in her social service endeavours. Her plan was that this woman would replace her in the pulpit while she was on the road. Rheba Crawford was the California State social welfare director, and was eight years younger than Aimee. She had an ability to hold crowds that was almost as compelling as Aimee's. Crawford was not only an experienced social services administrator; she was a former Protestant minister with Salvation Army roots. Crawford was the woman labelled the "Angel of Broadway" because she had preached to up to a thousand people in Times Square. Rheba was the one who inspired the hit musical, *Guys and Dolls*. Crawford had resigned from her church when she divorced and remarried. But with Aimee, she didn't have to worry about that. Aimee was in the same position she was. It seemed to be a match made in heaven for both of them.

Aimee set off on her evangelistic tours confidant that Crawford would take care of things at home. But although the Angel of Broadway did bring in the crowds, she had a political persuasion that was not compatible with Aimee's. Within months of hiring her, Aimee was getting reports from Roberta that Crawford was openly referring to public officials and mob members by name, and condemning their actions from the pulpit. Aimee had always been proud of her positive working relationship with the police department, state officials, and city hall. Now she was getting angry phone calls and letters from them.

Crawford refused to listen to reason, and went on condemning the same government she had worked for. When Crawford outright refused to stop, the temple board of directors requested her resignation. Crawford launched a lawsuit against the temple, claiming wrongful dismissal. Aimee knew then that even the governance of the temple was getting out of control.

Aimee had long ago decided that Rolf would someday run the administrative side of the operation. But he was not yet mature enough to handle the financial crisis or the law-suit with Crawford. Aimee had to have someone else keep the business running smoothly until Rolf was ready to take over. She looked to the fatherly Reverend Giles Knight, the man who was overseeing her Foursquare Gospel branch churches, to straighten out the mess. Knight had been Minnie's assistant when she returned to the temple to bail it out of its financial crisis a few years earlier. He was steady, strong, and reliable.

Knight instigated what Roberta called a "dictatorship." Knight put all the administrative staff of the temple on a tight budget. Where before they could access temple funds easily, he now made everyone adhere to a strict accounting system with checks and balances. Everyone was chaffing at the bit. Roberta sent a letter of protest to her mother. And Minnie, who, though absent, was always in the background when it came to Aimee's daughter, backed her up.

Roberta's complaints might not have riled Aimee too much, if Minnie had not become involved. Although she had never faced Aimee directly since their parting, Minnie made her presence felt through Roberta. From Aimee's point of view, Minnie refused to mind her own business regarding issues involving the temple. She had run it too long to totally give up her interest in it. It was Minnie's contention that the control of the operation should remain in family hands. Besides, in her opinion, Knight had been given too much authority. Minnie thought that Roberta should be given more control than Knight and told her granddaughter that.

Aimee had long resented the close alliance between her daughter and her mother. Roberta had always been closer to Minnie than she had been to her mother. Ever since Aimee had left Roberta with Minnie on the farm as a child while she went away to preach, Roberta had viewed Minnie as her number one role model. At 24 years old, the young divorcee appeared to be becoming just like Minnie. She had, for some time, tried to tell Aimee how to run the operation. Aimee may also have been worried that she and Minnie were forming a conspiracy against her. Obviously, the two of them were talking about Aimee behind her back on an ongoing basis. Was there a conspiracy to throw Aimee out of the temple? After all, Minnie had tried it once before.

Aimee, Rolf, and Roberta were the three principals of the Echo Park Evangelistic Association, the holding company for all of their assets. Aimee decided that the time had come to stand up for herself against her mother and Roberta. Subsequently, she talked to her son and Aimee and Rolf voted Roberta out. Aimee took over control of the entire enterprise.

Minnie then went to the press and told them that she felt that Aimee was doing to her daughter the same thing she had done to her 10 years before, that is pushing Roberta away in order to take control. It was Minnie's contention that

Aimee had "never been able to hold anyone close to her," and that in "casting out" her daughter, and separating herself from her family, she might "chart her own course to ruin."

It could be said that Aimee suffered from a mild form of paranoia. But it could also be said that she surrounded herself with people who thought in a particularly narrow way. In other words, she was drawn to people who had no ability to tolerate her open-mindedness, thereby creating the climate for her own rejection.

Meanwhile, Roberta was reeling from the blow, and when her mother insulted her, through her lawyer, the young woman was ready for a fight. A press release issued by Aimee's lawyer, Willedd Andrews, insinuated that Roberta had "intimidated, threatened, and blackmailed" her mother. Roberta sued her Aimee's lawyer for slander, and won a settlement of $2000.

Roberta used this money to move to New York, and went to work in broadcasting. Reverend Knight refused to allow Roberta access to Aimee, claiming that he was protecting Aimee from hostile influences. Only Rolf and his wife, along with a few other individuals, were allowed to enter Aimee's private life for the next eight years. He also refused to allow Aimee to travel outside Los Angeles to preach or to speak to the press. She was to remain at home, to rest, and to concentrate on rebuilding the temple. Within two years, in the height of the Great Depression, Knight had paid off more than $60,000 of the temple's debt.

After eight years of relative seclusion, Aimee put Rolf in charge of the Angelus Temple. At the age of 30 he assumed the role of vice president, and Knight, who was by this time more than ready to retire, resigned.

In September 1945, Aimee Semple McPherson and Rolf McPherson travelled to Oakland, California, to dedicate a new branch church. On the eve of the dedication, Aimee and Rolf talked late into the night in Aimee's hotel room. They discussed her plans for the expansion of the branch churches. Aimee was excited and exhilarated about Rolf's potential for demonstrating capable leadership.

But once Rolf returned to his room, Aimee could not calm down enough to sleep. Her mind was, as many times before, tumbling and jumbled with plans and dreams.

Aimee took out a vial of sedatives, poured them across her pillow, and put a few in her mouth. Hmm ... how many had she taken? She couldn't remember. She took another one, then another, and she thought she was starting to feel lighter. But the mattress was so hard, not like her soft bed at home ... not her bed ... strange bed ... strange people ... strange food ... strange sounds ... strange smells. How many pills would it take to fall asleep? Maybe one more. Was that too many? Why wouldn't the heaviness go away?

Aimee woke up suddenly — sweating, heart pounding, vision cloudy, tongue thick — something was wrong — terribly wrong. She fumbled in her purse to find her doctor's number. The contents of her purse spilled out across the floor: make-up, pens and pencils, peoples' phone numbers, prayer requests, scripture verses scribbled out on little pieces of paper. At last — the address book — there it was. She fell to her knees, picked it up and struggled to dial the number. Her fingers felt like sticks. "Hello? ... Hello? ... Hello? This is Aimee Semple McPherson ... Aimee ... Semple..."

Her doctor was in surgery. The voice on the phone gave her the number of another doctor. She tried to dial again, her fingers stiff. She struggled to make them move, but they were so thick and heavy. Dawn was breaking through her window. Then ... another voice on the phone ... someone was telling her to phone yet another doctor. She tired to make her fingers move again, but they refused, she could no longer hold the phone. Aimee fell across the bed, unconscious.

Pounding on the door. Pounding. Someone was shouting ... it sounded like Rolf ... shouting ... shouting ... so loud, but she couldn't wake up. He shook her. "Mother! Mother!" Nothing. Nothing. She couldn't hear anything. Pillows ... pillows ... so soft. Then ... silence.

Although Rolf rushed her to the hospital, the doctors could not resuscitate his mother. On September 27, 1944, at 11:45 a.m., Aimee Semple McPherson was pronounced dead.

Aimee had planned her funeral service years before. However, the funeral was delayed for two weeks to allow 1700 ministers, whom Aimee had personally ordained, to arrive from around the globe. Aimee's body lay on the stage of Angelus Temple, in a bronze casket, for three days. More than 50,000 mourners filed passed it. The temple was filled with flowers and the temple band played her favourite revival hymns. She had planned a three-hour service, to which Rheba Crawford came. The two battling ministers had settled their dispute out of court years before. Minnie could not bring herself to come to the service, but she did go to the cemetery. Roberta could not get a flight from New York, as military personnel had first bid on airplane seats in wartime. Harold McPherson took a series of buses from Florida and arrived on time for the service.

The day after the funeral, the three surgeons who had been conducting Aimee's inquest, finally decided to rule the death "accidental." There was talk of suicide. But due to her deteriorating health, failing kidneys, and relatively advanced age, the doctors decided to let the cause of her death remain an open-ended question.

And so, today, both the mind behind the great woman evangelist and her death remain a mystery.

Epilogue

The Church of the Foursquare Gospel, Aimee's international organization, has more than 37,000 churches and 52,000 ministers in 142 countries. Rolf McPherson continued to run the organization until his retirement in 1988. Angelus Temple is still operating across from Echo Park in Los Angeles.

Minnie died three years after Aimee. Her estate was estimated to have been worth several hundred thousand dollars, while Aimee's estate had an estimated cash value of $10,000. Roberta married Harry Salter, the creator, director, and producer of the television show *Name That Tune* in 1941, in New York City.

Aimee's healing ministry remained strong until the end of her life. She was reported to have had the most medically documented healings of any Christian minister up until her time.

Aimee Semple McPherson's interdenominational legacy led to the breaking down of the barriers between Christian groups. Her emphasis on love and charity helped to direct Christian churches in North America toward an emphasis on social justice and restoration.

Further Reading

Austin, Alvyn. *Aimee Semple McPherson*. Don Mills: Fitzhenry & Whiteside Limited, 1980.

Blumhofer, Edith L. *Aimee Semple McPherson — Everybody's Sister*. Grand Rapids: William B. Eerdmans Publishing Company, 1993.

Epstein, Daniel Mark. *Sister Aimee — The Life of Aimee Semple McPherson*. New York: Harcourt Brace Jovanovich Publishers, 1993.

McPherson, Aimee Semple. *Give Me My Own God*. New York: H. C. Kinsey & Company Inc., 1936.

McPherson, Aimee Semple. *This is That*. Los Angeles: Foursquare Publications, 1923.

Shaefer, Sylvia Anne. *Aimee Semple McPherson*. Philadelphia: Chelsea House Publishers, 2004.

This web site contains valuable information about the International Foursquare Gospel Church: *www.ondoctrine.com/10mcpher.htm*

This is the official web site of the International Foursquare Gospel Church: *www.foursquare.org*